Educational Leadership:
Policy Dimensions in the 21st Century

Educational Policy in the 21st Century

Bruce Anthony Jones, Series Editor

Volume 1: *Educational Leadership: Policy Dimensions in the 21st Century, 2000*
edited by Bruce Anthony Jones

Educational Leadership:
Policy Dimensions in the 21st Century

edited by Bruce Anthony Jones

 Ablex Publishing Corporation
Stamford, Connecticut

Library of Congress Cataloguing-in-Publication Data

Educational leadership: policy dimensions in the 21st century / edited by
    Bruce Anthony Jones
        p. cm.—(Educational policy in the 21st century ; v. 1)
    Includes bibliographical references and indexes.
    ISBN 1-56750-488-4 (cloth)—ISBN 1-56750-489-2 (pbk.)
    1. Educational leadership—United States. 2. Educational planning—United States.
3. Education and state—United States. I. Jones, Bruce Anthony. II. Series.

  LB2805.E3475 2000
  379.73—dc21   99-046145

Ablex Publishing Corporation
100 Prospect Street
P.O. Box 811
Stamford, Connecticut 06904-0811

CONTENTS

ACKNOWLEDGMENTS

This is to express appreciation to the members of the National Policy Board for Educational Administration (NPBEA) Policy Circle. The primary motivation for the development of this book is the result of discussion among the members of the NPBEA Policy Circle. The members of the NPBEA Policy Circle are James G. Cibulka, Robert Johnson, Carolyn D. Herrington, Carolyn Kelley, Betty Merchant, James Ward, Audrey Noble, Edward St. John, and Martha McCarthy. I have had the privilege to serve as coordinator of the Policy Circle.

The NPBEA Policy Circle was established in 1996 by the National Policy Board for Educational Administration Board to serve as the research entity to address policy issues emanating from the membership of the organizations that comprise the National Policy Board for Educational Administration Board. These organizations are the American Association of Colleges for Teacher Education; the American Association of School Administrators, the Council of Chief State Officers, the National Association of Elementary School Principals, the National Council of Professors of Educational Administration, the National School Boards Association, and the University Council for Educational Administration.

I also acknowledge Kathryn M. Borman, Professor of Education at the University of South Florida-Tampa who served as a critical inspiration for this book and the Ablex Educational Policy Series.

FOREWORD

As we look into the 21st century, there are many challenges to be faced in the field of education, both internal and external to schools, that will determine both what children learn and how they learn. In the absence of large-scale improvements in schooling in this country, we will continue to be concerned with improving instruction and learning, ensuring effectiveness of teachers, strengthening schools as institutions, preparing diverse populations for the future, and gaining a better understanding of the changing social context and what that means for individuals and the nation. The contributions provided in this book shed light on and initiate debates about important policy issues associated with education reform and improvement. The authors do this by linking conceptual frameworks to past research, analyzing these challenges, and speculating about the contours of future research and school practice.

When historians look back on education in the 20th century, I suspect they will argue that this was a unique period in the evolution of public education in the United States, particularly regarding the institutional forms that came into existence during this time period and the shifts in fundamental assumptions about how the enterprise is best governed and managed. It is appropriate that this volume opens its discussion by taking a poignant glance at the current stream of innovative ways of thinking about schools as organizations. Dissatisfaction with school effectiveness has, over the last decade or so, led to some experimentation with new forms of organization and governance. It is worth exploring the forces that give rise to the growing attraction of charter schools for instance, or the persistent call for vouchers. Clearly the existing architecture of central administration and local governance is seen as weak, unstable, or possibly even irrelevant to a growing number of parents and teachers. Yet with these new alternatives, it is important to ask whether these or current paradigms more effectively educate our children and prepare them for an increasingly dynamic, technological world.

This text next explores education policies that affect learning of diverse populations and ignites a discussion about who will be able to teach effectively and lead teachers to educate an ever-changing student population. Very often, children come to school with micro-environmental issues that, unquestionably, have an influence on what and how they learn. Many believe there is a growing need to build stronger bridges between schools and community organizations serving children and families. More than one chapter in this volume examines this question.

Important questions are also raised surrounding the details of school reform. Inevitably, when the topic of school reform is raised, government relationships, at the national and local level, and the efforts to implement systemic school reform naturally provoke debate. My own view is that there are inherent and important tensions between existing governance, organization, and management of schools with the idea of systemic education reform. I suspect that the growing private interest and involvement in public education is associated with this tension. This creates a need to examine what impact—if any—the private sector has made on improving schools and student performance. Two chapters in this volume delve into these types of questions.

Funding streams and sources are imperative issues to address when looking at education leadership and supporting changing systems within schools. What kinds of resources will schools require to meet the challenges of the 21st century? Of particular importance in analyzing resource questions is the "money doesn't matter" issue. The focus of this issue has traditionally centered on the battle between those who believe that money does make a difference and those who believe money does not make a difference. This book takes a fresh perspective and poses this question: "How" does money make a difference in advancing the mission of education?

Taken together, these themes and analyses speak volumes about the nature of leadership required in the 21st century if we are going to see the types of changes and improvements in American education we need to see. Leadership, I will argue, is the major factor in determining whether we will see change in this country to the scale of improvement needed to help, substantially, all the children achieve at high levels. Is this country prepared for the dynamics of changing demographics, increased globalization, and politics of mobilization that are characteristic of education trends in the 21st century? Who will lead this and future generations of change? What will it take for the United States to reach a state of leader preparedness? This book continues the spirited discussion on these and other challenges faced by researchers, practitioners, and policymakers. I highly commend it to you.

—C. Kent McGuire

part I
Educational Organizations: Evolving Thinking and Configurations

CONTESTS OVER GOVERNANCE OF EDUCATIONAL POLICY: PROSPECTS FOR THE NEW CENTURY

James G. Cibulka
University of Maryland

INTRODUCTION

As this chapter is written and the current century draws to a close, the governance of educational policy in elementary and secondary education is in a state of turmoil. Since the 1980s, governors and state legislatures have asserted ever more sweeping demands for reform of the educational system. In a number of American cities, mayors have sought to expand their influence over the public school system, reversing a period during the middle decades of the century when they shunned any responsibility for the schools. School boards and professional educators—both administrators and teachers—have found their traditional prerogatives questioned. Teachers unions, which fought hard to win the right to represent teachers to provide their members with better salaries and working conditions during the 1950s and 1960s, now find their values, and even their very legitimacy questioned. Further, the political base of support for public education, at one time guaranteed by a loyal middle-class and under represented minorities such as African Americans, is no longer certain. Many previously loyal public-school adherents, concerned about school safety and educational quality, have fled to private schools. Public support for vouchers, contracting, and charter schools is growing, as is the movement toward home schooling. In other words, the institutional arrangements and regimes that dominated educational policy making for much of this century are currently in disrepute.

This chapter examines the dominant debates about the shape of organizational and governance arrangements in the field of educational administration in the last century, describes developments in recent years, and speculates on the factors that are likely to influence how these debates are settled in the early part of the next century. This chapter focuses on the United States and on K–12 education. Although other national experiences certainly are relevant to these considerations, and higher education's governance presents vital choices for public policy, adequate attention to each of these issues would require another chapter.

GOVERNANCE IN TURMOIL

The early 20th century was a period during which the main outlines of today's educational governance arrangements for elementary and secondary education were set in place. It is useful to summarize these arrangements as institutional, as employed by theorists of the new institutionalism (e.g., March & Olsen, 1989; Powell & Dimagio, 1991). These ideas have been applied to education by a number of writers (e.g., Boyd, Crowson, & Macwhinney, 1996; Meyer & Rowan, 1977). I have applied this framework elsewhere (Cibulka, 1995; 1996) to illustrate how public schools have developed formal institutional structures to legitimatize their existence with key stakeholders in their environment. Similarly, regime theorists (e.g., Stone, 1998) show how formal and informal governance arrangements empower certain key actors and interests.

The institutional and regime arrangements advanced by the progressive reform movement in the first two decades of the 20th century favored a degree of centralization and professionalization previously unknown in the new enterprise of public schooling (Tyack, 1974). In the late 19th century, American public schooling was a highly local matter, kept in the hands of school boards whose members often represented very specific constituencies within each school community or neighborhood. Local politicians also had much to say about what was taught, who would be hired and fired, how the schools would be funded, and other critical policy questions. In cities, political machines often brokered jobs, lucrative contracts, real estate, and other political resources to build and maintain their power and legitimacy. Progressives sought to rationalize and expand the reach of this new public school enterprise by introducing business values of efficiency, turning over power to civic elites who supposedly had the broad public interest at heart, and handing authority for running the public schools to a new cadre of education professionals. School boards, while preferably elected under progressive doctrine, were to become smaller in size and were to confine their role to that of setting policy, much like a corporate board of directors. In order to assure that a broader perspective emerged, school board members were to be elected at-large rather than from wards or subdistricts. The election was to be held at a separate time to assure that the electoral process for school board members would be unsullied by partisan politics. Superintendents were to be given authority for instructional programs and business management and were seen as implementing the policy directions set by a school board, which was to be a trustee of the public interest, rather than a collection of individuals representing narrow self-interested constituencies. In this new regime, progressives were certain that there would be no need for politics because all matters could be resolved through the application of technical expertise. Corruption would be controlled by rendering its claims within policy setting obsolete. This new polity of experts and enlightened citizens would rule by consensus, reducing the fractious conflict that progressives observed as a too common feature of the growing urbanization of America.

Whatever its virtues, critics of this strategy of institutionalization have pointed to its social biases. This was a largely Protestant movement, nativist and small-town in its support, and one bent on preventing the takeover of public schools (and American society in general) by immigrants, who were viewed as a threat to American society. Moreover, it was a regime relying heavily on business to solidify its power base and to legitimatize it. Yet, depending on local circumstances, broad coalitions also emerged as advocates of the new "one best system," as Tyack (1974) describes this ideology. In some cities labor and business were allies; elsewhere they were members of different coalitions. Regardless of the specifics, a wide variety of interests turned to the new developing institution of public education as a way of achieving their social, economic, and political objectives. For some employee groups, it was an employment regime. For certain business interests, the public schools were sources of profit and a source of labor supply; and so on.

This progressive vision, ambitious as it was, could not be realized fully, of course. Some jurisdictions retained elements of the old political and representative system of school governance, and sometimes reforms had to be obtained piecemeal with much struggle against vested interests. Mayors still held sway in some cities, such as Baltimore and Chicago, where they largely controlled the appointed school boards. Local superintendents were still elected in states such as Florida. Superintendents did not always have full jurisdiction over all aspects of operations, particularly business. In Maryland, as well as local jurisdictions in many places of the country, school budgets remained under control of general-purpose governments.

Despite these irregularities and vestiges of the old order, however, the progressive reform agenda enjoyed remarkable success. Most school boards became politically and fiscally independent, most became smaller, and most gave superintendents broad authority. Professional bureaucracies grew in size and importance, lessening the power of school boards as well as the lay electorate. School systems were consolidated to overcome taxing inequities and grew in size to accommodate both a burgeoning population and the expansion of secondary schooling. By the middle decades of this century in many parts of the nation, the progressive promise of reform seemed to its longstanding supporters to have been fulfilled.

Even though the progressive formula eventually began to unravel, it is hard to overestimate its success. In the decades following World War II support for public schools was so strong that a massive school construction program was undertaken, seeking to accommodate the migration of blacks from the rural south to the northern cities, and to satisfy a growing middle-class migrating to expanding suburbs. Large numbers of new teachers were hired, teachers salaries improved to a degree, class sizes fell, and many special services came to be provided at the urging of a demanding public and school professionals.

Not everyone shared equally in this post-war educational expansion. Race continued to play a major role in American education, a problem which had never been adequately understood or addressed by progressives. The south continued to operate a dual school system even after the *Brown* decision in 1954, which unleashed a revolution of rising expectations for black Americans. Northern cities proved to be anything but refuges from the legacy of racial inequality, in many cases maintaining racially separate "neighborhood schools" with inferior facilities, staffing, and other educational opportunities. Cities became poorer as a result of suburbanization, losing their middle-class base and becoming unable to compete with their suburban counterparts for well-qualified teachers.

Social conflict erupted in many schools in the 1960s as a result of challenges brought by civil rights groups seeking desegregation or greater racial autonomy. Legal battles, which had begun in the 1950s, led to intervention by the courts, in some cases placing entire school systems under the supervision of a court monitor or judge. By the late 1960s, the Vietnam War and the demands of local communities for educational reforms of one kind or another added another layer of social conflict to the increasingly beleaguered educational enterprise. The consensual basis upon which progressive governance had rested was put to its most severe test since the inception of the new ideology. Many school officials were unprepared to manage the conflict, which they had been socialized to believe was illegitimate.

The collective mobilization of teachers to bargain posed a parallel challenge to the legitimacy of a governance system resting on assumptions of a unitary public interest. Collective bargaining, as adapted from trade unionism, began from the assumption that labor and management have separate and incompatible interests (Kerchner & Koppich, 1997). Although most southern and some western states resisted unionization, in much of the country, teacher unions won the right to represent teachers. Although collective bargaining laws differ widely, over time, many school boards gave up considerable discretion and both parties came to view one another as adversaries. Moreover, the power of big teachers unions to strike was used indiscriminately in some jurisdictions like Chicago, where teachers were part of the mayoral regime, eventually causing public resentment to reach such heights that teachers' powers were sharply curbed by the Illinois state legislature in 1988 and 1995 (Shipps, 1998).

Other political challenges were added to the twin pincers of racial unrest and unionization. Educational research (Coleman et al., 1966) began to question whether or not schools could be the agent of social change that many reformers had assumed them to be, leading many fiscal conservatives to question further investments in public education. In the 1970s, public school educators faced declining enrollments for the first time since the Second World War. They came under sustained attack for failing to reduce expenditures, and in some states and local jurisdictions fell victim to tax and spending limitations.

The advent of Ronald Reagan's presidency signaled a shift in the national mood toward less government and a reversal of federal power. Urban school systems, in particular, suffered large cutbacks in federal aid, although Reagan failed to achieve his goal of consolidating all federal categorical programs. The publication of *A Nation at Risk* in 1983 moved educational policy toward a new emphasis defined by concern for efficiency, productivity, and accountability. The involvement of Presidents Bush and Clinton in school reform issues signaled that the nation's civic and political elites, as well as its academic establishment, regarded education as a top domestic policy priority. Led by political forces outside the educational establishment, this new reform nostrum eventually came to question some of the basic assumptions of governance, which had been unthinkable heresy only two decades earlier. The autonomy traditionally accorded professional educators lessened in the face of this new political activism on the part of elected political leaders. Their opinions, while not ignored, were no longer taken at face value. In particular, the ascendancy of a growing conservative movement provided a durable opposition to much educational orthodoxy—that more school spending will improve student achievement, that educators can be trusted to develop sound curricula, that teachers are well qualified and always have the children's best interests at heart, that private schools do not deserve taxpayer support, and so on. If educational progressivism is not entirely dead in the 1990s—its institutional apparatus still is largely intact— its normative claims had been so sharply undercut that its legitimacy and ultimate survival could well be questioned.

SOURCES OF DISPUTE CONCERNING GOVERNANCE CHOICES

Given the political developments previously discussed, it is likely that public education's governance will be significantly restructured in the early decades of the new millennium, or at the very least that contests over the shape of governance will be a major part of the politics of education. In this section, we review the major parameters that are likely to be in dispute. Political scientists and other students of government will recognize many of these issues as perennial. Six issues are cited as follows.

The Degree of Decentralization (e.g., Devolution, Deregulation) in Intergovernmental Relations

The American system of divided powers exists not only between the branches of government but among levels. By constitutional design, education is a state function, not a federal one (Peterson, 1995). Moreover, by tradition (except for the anomalous case of Hawaii), the delivery of education has been delegated to local school districts. Both the state and federal government's roles have been subjects of periodic controversy. Through most of the century, state power over local school districts has expanded. There has not been a one-to-one correspondence between the level of state funding and degree of state regulation when one makes comparisons between states. There is, however, a widespread perception that with greater state support, state control has increased. At the same time, some have questioned the assumption that greater state regulation necessarily leads to loss of local control (Fuhrman & Elmore, 1990). This debate is not likely to be resolved empirically, however, because proponents of greater centralization or decentralization often call upon different political philosophies and ideologies. Those who favor greater decentralization often cite the virtues of a Jeffersonian vision of a republican polity centered around neighborhoods and communities, which arguably emphasizes responsiveness and civic virtue. Those favoring strong central government institutions—the focus on state or federal governments varies, depending on the issue in question—see advantages in terms of efficiency and equity. Perhaps the main rationale for a strong federal role in education has been to provide greater equity and local capacity to compensate for local and regional differences in wealth and support for public education. Proposals for national standards and tests in the Clinton administration have gotten caught in the crossfire between proponents of centralization (in this case in the supposed interest of improving quality) and the decentralizers, who fear federal control of curricula.

Another thread in this debate concerns the issue of heavily regulatory federal and state education programs. Critics have complained that state and federal governments often add unfunded mandates or they provide aid with so many strings attached that the programs cannot fit local priorities and needs. In 1999, Congress passed a law deregulating many federal categorical programs. For many staunch advocates of deregulation, however, this is not enough. They favor total decategorization of federal programs and substituting them with block grants providing general aid. If this were to happen, many of the socially redistributive federal programs would disappear, although more of the block grants might still be targeted to districts in greatest need. Thus, decentralization and deregulation are not identical reform nostrums. Some who favor retaining a federal role favor greater deregulation of federal programs, although few would totally dismantle key federal initiatives such as the Elementary and Secondary Education Act.

Control Through Special Purpose Versus General Purpose Governments (Mayors and Common Councils, and County Officials)

Progressive reformers, as was explained earlier, made the case for being treated as a separate unit of government because, they argued, education differs from other local services. The technical, professional nature of education requires that it be governed and administered nonpolitically.

Recent efforts by big-city mayors in Boston, Chicago, and New York to increase their authority run directly counter to the progressive formula of political independence. For decades, mayors were only too happy to comply with at least the trappings of progressive orthodoxy, even if they exercised political influence over school board elections and other aspects of school system operations from behind the scenes. In that period, the belief in schools as a reform enterprise was so pervasive that the costs of becoming overtly involved in school affairs were too high. School issues often provoke intensely emotional reactions from parents, thus making it a risky political venture for elected politicians. In recent years, however, the political calculus has changed. Mayors view education as central to the economic well-being and development of their metropolis and a key resource in attracting and retaining businesses and an educated citizenry. Public concern over school quality also is so grave that mayors who do not make reform of the public schools a platform for their administration risk criticism from opponents, the press, and the public.

The question remains, however, whether or not the involvement of mayoral leadership in the schools is, on balance, a good thing. Jurisdictions where county councils and executives hold the purse strings over schools often witness increased politicization of educational issues. School administrators complain that the schools become political footballs attached to other political agendas, and school issues become bargaining chips in a larger game of regime politics, particularly efforts by elected politicians wishing to take credit for keeping taxes down.

Here again, there is no clear answer to which governance arrangement is in the best interests of the citizenry. Are politically independent school systems any less subject to political influence? Do not teachers unions, which are arguably a special interest group, often exercise great influence over who is elected to school boards? There is a school of thought among political scientists that formal institutional arrangements, while they do make a difference in political outcomes, are less important than the values of the citizenry. Where education is valued, so goes the logic, support for the public schools is likely to occur regardless of the formal governance arrangements. Even if that assertion is true, reformers can claim that changing authority from special purpose to general purpose government, or vice versa, will improve the schools. In essence, they are making a claim to control by a new set of authorities, more than the structural advantages of one or the other institutional arrangement.

The Shifting Balance Between Public and Private Ownership, Control, and Management

In the 1990s, a serious debate began to emerge over whether or not government should be the dominant provider of public education. Cannot private schools, whose patrons are supported with vouchers or tax credits, operate in the public interest? If this were to occur, it would reverse a hallmark of the progressive nostrum, which was guided by a vision of "one best system" under public ownership and operation.

While private schools have been gaining market share in the United States, the constitutional separation of church and state has been a formidable obstacle to their receiving state support. Nevertheless, constitutional scholars weigh in on both sides of this issue. The United States Supreme Court declined to rule on the constitutionality of the Milwaukee school choice program, which was upheld by the Wisconsin Supreme Court in 1998. Even if aid to religious schools is not upheld, the possibility of aid for attendance at nonsectarian private schools would remain.

Public opinion may be an important factor weighing in the balance, since courts are not entirely oblivious to the social context of their rulings. In this regard, until recently, public opinion was very divided and more opposed than supportive of the concept of vouchers or tax credits. Even though the specific wording of opinion poll questions yields somewhat different pluralities, a majority of the public, including African Americans, now favor vouchers. This signals a significant change in the public's willingness to entertain other ways to deliver public education. Public school advocates worry that this shift in the public mood represents willingness of the middle-class to abandon public education.

Other forms of school choice may also be open to adoption. Charter schools in some jurisdictions would permit contracts with private providers and already are underway in some places. School boards are interested in contracting with private providers, such as Sylvan Learning Systems, to deliver some of their educational program. This approach retains oversight of the programs with the local board of education, which is not necessarily the case with charter schools.

Teachers unions are among the biggest opponents of choice arrangements involving some kind of privatization, although the National Education Association has expressed qualified endorsement for charter schools that meet their approval criteria. Demand for greater attention by the teacher unions to issues of educational quality comes partly from the ranks of teachers themselves. Many teachers, particularly younger, new entrants to the field, expect their union to be a more forceful advocate for education reform and to assist them in making improvements to their teaching and the schools where they work.

In the 1980s, as the education reform movement picked up momentum, proposals by President Reagan to "voucherize" E.S.E.A. Chapter 1 programs were considered radical and extremist. By the late 1990s, private school choice became a major option under debate. The country had moved further to the right politically, signaled by Republican majorities in both houses of the United States Congress. School vouchers have become a major policy goal of Republicans at the national, state, and local levels, in some cases with support from Democrats.

Professional Autonomy Versus External Accountability

No established profession in modern society is entirely self-regulating. Thus, there is considerable debate about how much autonomy is appropriate, and how public accountability should be exercised. The state plays an important role in deciding what the qualifications are for licensure of professionals. Frequently, professional guilds work closely with government officials to set standards for entrance and satisfactory performance, and for disciplining professionals whose performance falls below acceptable standards. From an institutional perspective, both professional groups and government can benefit from this collaborative relationship. Unregulated professional guilds, and the excesses and abuses they could be expected to spawn, would threaten the legitimacy of both the state and the profession. In particular, professionals often find an ally in government in promulgating standards of practice they consider desirable or vital to the public interest.

Two factors have increased the demands for greater accountability—declining satisfaction with public school performance and the mobilization of political conservatives. The latter, for example, challenge the idea that current licensure standards for teachers protect quality. These critics charge that restrictions on entry in the profession are monopolistic, and although they benefit the profession, they impose costs on society by restricting the entry of talented individuals to the field and by driving up salaries.

Demands to increase the accountability of the educational system should be viewed in this political context. School professionals were never totally free of public oversight. State legislatures set standards, and school boards often enforce local community mores, both of which provide checks on professional discretion to serve the client (here, the student). The progressive movement tipped the balance in favor of far greater autonomy for the new guild of superintendents and other school administrators than had been the case in the past. Willingness to grant this autonomy almost always is conditional, however. It depends on the trust of clients and the public. As long as the education profession could hold itself out as champions of progress and protectors of the child's best interests, a platform upon which it made credible claims for most of this century, autonomy and professionalism could go hand in hand. Recently, decline of trust in governmental institutions, and in particular dissatisfaction with the performance of public schools, has reinvigorated interest in accountability as a value in representative democracy.

In recent years, there have been efforts to make teaching and school administration more professional through standard setting processes such as the Interstate

New Teacher Assessment and Support Consortium (INTASC) and the Interstate School Leaders Licensure Consortium (ISLLC), which will guide both licensure tests and program reviews for institutions of higher education. National certification for teachers also is in the early stages of implementation. These efforts often are defended as making the profession more accountable for performance standards. In other words, professionalization can proceed on a parallel path with the state's demands for greater accountability. An institutional perspective helps us see that both professional groups and government (elected political officials as well as bureaucrats) increase, or at least maintain, their legitimacy by working together. Yet within these symbiotic relationships, the broad tension remains. To what extent are teachers and administrators to be given the autonomy to apply professional standards in the conduct of their work? Critics of the current education reform movement see within it a tendency to devalue teachers as bearers of intellectual property and instead increasingly to ask them to implement policy agendas that emerge external to their influence and contrary to their best judgement. Attempts to give schools greater autonomy and free them from regulation may counterbalance this trend, but so far, these contrary trends have been weaker.

Were school choice and privatization to expand as elements of a new governance regime, this development would be interpreted as an expansion of external accountability. Would this development in the direction of market-based accountability increase incentives for professionalization, or would it push in the direction of further deprofessionalization? A number of scenarios might be envisioned. Greater choice in the form of charter schools, vouchers, and so forth, could give teachers, as well as principals, greater control over their workplace and expand conditions wherein professional autonomy could be exercised, quite unlike the rudimentary efforts contained in site-based management. At the same time, possible loss of power by teachers unions over collective bargaining contracts and greater flexibility in state licensure requirements allowing nontraditional means of gaining professional licensure, could undermine efforts to raise professional standards. These are not mutually exclusive options; they could occur simultaneously. Also, trends exogenous to the school choice controversy, such as the much discussed teacher and administrator shortage at the end of the century, could accelerate pressures to lift entry standards into the profession.

When public dissatisfaction with institutional performance rises, accountability is seen as a way of improving results. Hence, accountability measures focus on publication of student test scores and attaching policy consequences to the results in the form of rewards and sanctions. Teachers and administrators working in school systems where school performance is perceived as poor are likely to have their school placed on probation, see the school closed, or even to lose their jobs. Thus, the tension between professional autonomy and external accountability is likely to endure and possibly, even be exacerbated in the years ahead.

Family Versus Community Control

While there is a long tradition of local control of public education in the United States, it has been seen as a public function controlled by the community. Debates over local and state control or local and federal control are merely contests over which community of interest should dominate policy setting. It is true, of course, that advocates for local control have long made a strong claim that the local community is closest to the family and that other institutions geographically situated in the neighborhood or nearby, such as religious and social service organizations, are in the best position to understand the child's needs. The more remote the level of government is from the child, so the argument goes, the less policy makers are in a position to understand the cultural needs of that child or to respond appropriately. Those who argue for state and national roles in education often cite that inequities flow from such excess localism, given differences of fiscal capacity among communities, differences in willingness to support public education, and tendencies toward ethnic and racial prejudice where one group holds dominant power in local communities.

The rekindling of interest in family control of schooling turns this argument on its head and pronounces all of the previous arguments wrong. The family is the appropriate unit for deciding what is in the best interests of the child, by affording the family choice of school. The expansion of public education systems was an effort to displace the family as the central decision making unit for education. The rationale was that changes in the economic order away from a craft and guild system toward industrialization had changed not only the family structure but also educational opportunities available within the home. The legitimate role for parents to shape education for their children necessarily lessened. The public schools also sought to socialize immigrants, whose level of literacy and values were questioned by those groups who controlled the new educational system. In practice, the middle and upper classes have been more advantaged than the poor in advancing their family values through their influence in the community.

Today, family choice in education is advocated as a way of protecting family values and introducing more incentives for schools to be responsive to those familial expectations. The growth of the home schooling movement in the United States is another expression of the suspicion of the capacity and willingness of public schools to respond to those family values.

The ideal of community that emerges from this conception is a far more attenuated one than that to be found within the tradition of local control. Community is based on voluntary affiliation around shared needs. The legitimate right to coerce a child and his or her family on the basis of a community's conception of what is in the "public" interest is rejected. The only contract between a family and a broader community is one into which the family enters willingly. It is not defined by geographically proximity but rather by shared taste, values, or needs, and it is revocable when that common interest is no longer shared by the parties. This

conception of community as one of shared opportunity rather than shared obligation is, by some interpretations, a postmodern response to the advent of multina-
tional, global institutions.

There are, of course, arguments against this family choice perspective. Not all
children have intact families, and not all parents care enough about their children
to act on behalf of their best interests. Even well-intentioned parents have limited
information and may make mistaken choices. The community should have some
voice in rearing a child because a democracy requires a citizenry with shared
respect for democratic values. Public education, for some of its advocates, is a
forum for creating a community of dialogue and an arena of struggle for a more
caring and just society.

This argument is one of the central axes in the current debate over school choice.
In practice, of course, choice arrangements can be a compromise between family
and community control. The state can regulate educational choices individual
families make. Highly regulated systems of choice could even expand family
choice for some while shrinking it for others (if large numbers of private schools
come under public regulation). Thus, even if school choice is expanded, there will
be a continuing debate over the role of families in determining educational
opportunities, and which community of interests should influence or constrain
those family choices.

"Shared" Versus Hierarchical Management by Educational Leaders

The internal management of educational organizations has been a key source of
disagreement in the politics of education. Collective bargaining of teachers, as
mentioned earlier, was one of the major disputes of the post-World War II period
(roughly 1945–1975). Teacher unionism prevailed in many parts of the country,
beginning with the first collective bargaining law in Wisconsin. Both the American
Federation of Teachers and the National Education Association, the two major
national organizations, adopted an industrial unionism model. The premises of this
model are, among other things, that labor and management have irreconcilable
differences of interest and that teacher unionism should confine itself to the
protection of wages, benefits, and working conditions favorable to its members.
The issue of improving quality of the enterprise was outside this calculus. As labor
unions in the private sector were forced to adapt to changes in the economy and the
growing power of their business employers, pressures on teacher unions to change
also came. This pressure was fueled by public expectations that schools need to
improve their performance. Thus, the advent of the new unionism represents an
attempt by leaders of the American Federation of Teachers and the National
Education Association to adapt to a new set of pressures.

The new unionism, however, is fraught with unanswered questions, which union
traditionalists seize upon in resisting change. Many of these issues revolve around
uncertainty over management's good intentions. If teachers agree to sit on site-

based school councils, will they absolve management of some of its responsibilities? If teachers agree to evaluate their peers, will they be doing the work that management should be doing? If issues of quality are part of the collective bargaining process, will teachers sacrifice salary advances, benefits, and favorable working conditions, which traditionally they fought for and won?

Many of these fears are grounded in adverse experiences unions have had with management. Many superintendents and their administrative staffs, as well as school boards, continue to emphasize administrative control over collaboration. Thus, it is easy to justify and reproduce earlier working relationships unless teachers, administrators, and boards are willing to take risks together.

New conceptions of administrative leadership emphasize the role of the principal and superintendent as leaders who facilitate leadership by teachers and work collaboratively with a wide range of actors, including teachers. These ideas influence preparation programs for school leaders. The conception that schools should be structured as learning organizations and communities of learners also is gaining greater acceptance. Such a philosophy focuses upon teachers as collaborators around improvement of their schools, particularly as these efforts focus on improving learning for all students. It rests upon a recognition that schools and school systems have organizational cultures that are powerful and can either impede or sustain educational restructuring. Thus, the new unionism appears to be one strand among a number of parallel lines of thinking. A convergence among these could lead to a new acceptance of shared approaches to educational management.

These parameters concerning educational governance are likely to remain unsettled issues for several reasons. First, they reflect deep-seated values in our political culture, which receive different degrees of emphasis over time, depending on the problems the nation is facing, the political parties and coalitions in power, and so on. Second, these issues are a means of asserting control over educational resources, processes, and outcomes, and thus are used by protagonists to their advantage. Third, although there is an evolving knowledge base about the effectiveness of one or another governance approach to resolving each of these questions, such knowledge is always being revised and, in any event, must always be qualified by contextual differences.

INSTITUTIONALISM AND POLITICAL MOBILIZATION PERSPECTIVES ON GOVERNANCE REFORM

I have reviewed six sources of tension surrounding educational governance. The ways in which these tensions are resolved clearly vary across national contexts, across policy domains within a nation, (e.g., K–12 education compared with higher education), and over time within a particular policy context, such as K–12 education.

What are the underlying political dynamics driving the way these enduring tensions are articulated, and the ways in which they are resolved? One way to characterize these dynamics is to draw a contrast between two quite different political processes. One of these we have described in some detail as the political force that shaped American K–12 education—institutionalism. Institutional forms can be understood as both structural and symbolic responses designed to assure goal achievement, survival, and legitimacy for the institution. (For a more complete exposition of this approach to institutionalism, see Cibulka, 1995.) Institutions are affected by the larger *societal environment*, which is characterized by such diverse phenomena as demographic shifts, flows of capital, residential patterns, shifts in values, changes in political regimes, and international influences. The institution consists also of an *organizational structure* (formal and informal), attendant policies, practices, norms, and legitimating myths affecting goal achievement, survival, and legitimacy. Feedback loops link the societal environment, institutional environment, and organizational structure.

This institutional model helps us to see that institutions are not only shaped by exogenous forces in their societal environments. In addition, they help shape the societal environment, and in particular, their own institutional environment in order to advance their goal achievement, survival, and legitimacy. The degree to which the institution is a dominant force, however, depends heavily on the quality of the leadership in the institution. There are few, if any, clear signals from the environment. Hence, the skill with which these developments in the societal and institutional environments are recognized and managed helps determine how stable the institution will be in periods of change, or whether the institution will carry within it the seeds of its own instability or even destruction.

In the United States, much of the 20th century was characterized by institutional hegemony. This is because public school educators were able to build an institutional apparatus with broad public support. The legitimating myth that politics and education are separate helped to insulate public education from its critics. So did the myth that public education promotes equal opportunity and widening social opportunity for American citizens. Fueled by an expanding population for much of the century, public-school educators were able to build a supportive institutional environment in which they exerted great influence over policy, as well as how policy was shaped and implemented through governance.

Challenges to these authoritative and exchange relationships in the institutional environment must come from changing societal forces largely exogenous to the institution. They are, therefore, disruptions to the status-quo by virtue of presenting new problems or new demands for policy participation. We refer to these challenges as *the politics of mobilization*. In contrast to the politics of institutionalization, which are driven by largely distributive benefits to the institutional actors, mobilization involves redistribution of authority or perquisites. As suggested previously, how the institution responds to these destabilizing forces is crucial. Inept responses can lead to further demands for change and potentially fundamental changes in the institution, if not its demise. Skillful management of mobilization, on the other hand, can reinforce the institution's dominant hand. For example, the civil rights movement broadened participation in school politics for African Americans and later for other racial or ethnic minorities, from which they accrued specific policy benefits as well. Despite many examples of short-term lapses of leadership in responding to civil rights challenges, over the long term, the institution was able to absorb these potentially destabilizing claims upon its legitimacy and survival. It did so by accommodating moderate demands for greater minority representation on school boards and in the teaching and administrative cadre, while rejecting the more extreme demands for "community control" of schools and "black power." In this way, the institution avoided any requirement that it make fundamental changes in governance. This example underscores the fact that the ultimate resolution of political mobilization may lead to further strengthening of the institution's dominance within its environment.

Yet, these larger political forces emergent from the societal environment always have a revolutionary potential. For example, in recent decades, shifts in the nature of the American economy and their concomitant international repercussions, have posed the most significant challenge to the established order of public schooling (e.g., Weeres & Kerchner, 1996). The engagement of the nation's civic and political elites in issues of school reform has reduced the ability of public school educators to dominate the framing of problems and solutions. These elites, if anything, pose more of a challenge than the mass protest challenges of the 1960s and 1970s because they come from elites with a power base of their own and with wide influence in a variety of other institutions, including the media.

The shift toward political conservatism in the larger societal environment also introduces demands for greater accountability, which already has led to new forms of governance relying on family choice, use of performance information, application of rewards and sanctions for performance, and a host of other business-oriented ideas that had little place in the old established institutional order of public schooling. Indeed, governance responses to perceived problems of performance often serve as quick palliatives or symbolic responses designed to reassure the public that something is being done to "solve" a vexing problem.

The dynamics of institutional growth are fueled by what has been called institutional isomorphism (Meyer & Rowan, 1977), in which institutional forms are mimicked and lead to a kind of organizational uniformity. Similarly, in periods when demands for institutional change are intense, the "copycat" syndrome can cause policies, like reconstitution of failing schools, to spread like wildfire from one state to another, thus leading to a new kind of institutional isomorphism, quite independent of any concrete evidence that these responses are anything more than symbolic.

Thus, the central unanswered question for the politics of K–12 education at the turn of the century is whether or not governance will be characterized by the dynamics of institutionalism or political mobilization. The former is likely to lead to only marginal shifts along the six governance dimensions discussed in this chapter. The politics of mobilization will lead to significant modifications in at least some, if not all, of the six established institutional parameters, since they are in many respects interrelated.

Public school educators, as has been emphasized, are not limited to a strategy of merely reacting to outside forces. Institutional actors have a great deal of influence in deciding how to respond to societal trends and can manage these challenges with differing degrees of skill. Here one is reminded of Argyris and Schon's (1996) distinction between organizations that employ single versus double-loop learning. They are, in the first instance, limited to strategic responses that accommodate the status quo rather than having the capacity to generate new approaches and solutions focused on the underlying causes of the problems. Organizations that are accustomed to dominating policy find it difficult to make this transition to double-loop learning, for it requires relinquishing defensive routines and obsession with maintaining control, which interfere with genuine problem solving.

The ambiguity surrounding how to interpret environmental challenges complicates the task of responding intelligently to demands for institutional reform. For example, whereas some see charter schools as a sensible reform that is less odious than the dangers that a voucher system would entail, other stalwart defenders of the status quo resist charter schools as a fundamental encroachment on the tradition of public schooling. Both a lack of a consensus on the need to change, and differences of opinion about which reforms are strategically wise, inhibit the capacity of the institution for change.

Institutional forms carry their own conservatism. Existing constitutional arrangements and tradition both impose brakes on change. Thus, centralization is unlikely to proceed too far in the American context, just as extreme decentralization is likely to be challenged on constitutional grounds or by calling on the protagonists' interpretation of the American "tradition" of educational governance.

It is important to note, however, that dynamics within institutions make change possible. This is because, at any point in time, the governance of the institutional order is in an uneasy equilibrium. Tensions within the six governance dimensions and among them, once the status-quo is challenged, carry the seeds of disequilibrium. This centripetal tendency is reinforced by the fact that not all of the proposals for governance reform push for change in the same direction. Some trends are centralizing in their thrust (e.g., accountability), some decentralizing (e.g. vouchers), and some ambivalent, encouraging movement in both directions at once (e.g., greater professional autonomy). This makes it difficult to predict with certainty how educational governance will reshape itself.

If one were to hazard a guess, it will be a trend toward increasingly complex governance arrangements that combine significant features of *both* centralizing and decentralizing forces, but in novel ways. Also, there is likely to be a less coherent, more variegated set of institutional arrangements across the states and nation—different mixes of public and private, new forms of regulation, and a variety of ways of involving parents and students in educational decision making.

This greater complexity and variety (differentiation) will represent the continuing institutionalization of elementary and secondary education that has been occurring for most of this century. The institutional form, however, may evolve into something very different from the progressive reform model that dominated this century. The period ahead, in other words, will be one of experimentation and competition among competing forms.

Public school educators may help to reshape the institution by their willingness to experiment with new institutional forms, but they are unlikely to preserve the "one best system" as we have known it. Indeed, a strategy of resistance to changes in governance designed to preserve the old institutional order is likely to further weaken the institution's capacity to achieve its goals, and to maintain its legitimacy and survival. In such a scenario, the forces of political mobilization, rooted in macrosocietal changes already underway, are likely to greatly change the institutional environment of the public school enterprise and its organizational structures.

Given the power of the societal changes that are discussed in this chapter, in particular changes in the economy and the growth of political conservatism, major changes to education governance seem inevitable. But will it be reform or revolution? The politics of institutionalization will bring modifications to governance, while the politics of mobilization carry the potential for its fundamental transformation into a new institution.

REFERENCES

Argyris, C., & Schon, D. A. (1996). *Organizational learning II: Theory, method, and practice.* Reading, MA: Addison-Wesley.

Boyd, W. L., Crowson, R. L., & Macwhinney, H. B. (1996). *The politics of education and the new institutionalism: Reinventing the public school.* New York: Falmer Press.

Cibulka, J. G. (1996). The reform and survival of American public schools: An institutional perspective. In W. L. Boyd, R. L. Crowson, & H. B. Mawhinney (Eds.), *The politics of education and the new institutionalism: Reinventing the public school* (pp. 7–22). New York: Falmer Press.

Cibulka, J. G. (1995). The institutionalization of public schools: The decline of legitimating myths and the politics of organizational instability. In R. T. Ogawa (Ed.), *Advances in research and theories of school management and educational policy* (Vol. 3, pp. 123–158). Greenwich, CT: JAI Press.

Coleman, J. S., Campbell, E. O., Hobson, C., McPartland, J., Mood, A., Winfield, F., & York, R. (1966). *Equality of educational opportunity.* Washington, DC: United States Government Printing Office.

Fuhrman, S. H., & Elmore, R. F. (1990). Understanding local control in the wake of state education reform. *Educational Evaluation and Policy Analysis 12*(1), 82–96.

Kerchner, C. T., & Koppich, J. E. (1997). *United mind workers: Unions and teaching in the knowledge society.* San Francisco: Jossey-Bass.

March, J. G., & Olsen, J. P. (1989). *Rediscovering institutions: The organizational basis of politics.* New York: Free Press.

Meyer, J. W., & Rowan, B. (1977). Institutionalized organizations: Formal structure as myth and ceremony. *American Journal of Sociology 83,* 340–363.

Peterson, P. E. (1995). *The price of federalism.* Washington, DC: The Brookings Institution.

Powell, W. W., & Dimagio, P. J. (1991). *The new institutionalism in organizational analysis.* Chicago: University of Chicago Press.

Shipps, D. (1998, October). Regime change: Mayoral takeover of the Chicago Public Schools. Unpublished manuscript, Consortium on Chicago School Research, University of Chicago.

Stone, C. N. (Ed.). (1998). *Changing urban education.* Lawrence: University of Kansas Press.

Tyack, D. (1974). *The one best system: A history of American urban education.* Cambridge: Harvard University Press.

Weeres, J. G., & Kerchner, C. T. (1995). This time it's serious: Post-industrialism and the coming institutional change in education. In W. L. Boyd, R. L. Crowson, & H. B. Macwhinney (Eds.), *The politics of education and the new institutionalism: Reinventing the public school* (pp. 135–152). New York: Falmer Press.

2

PRIVATIZATION OF EDUCATION: MARKETPLACE MODELS

Martha McCarthy
Indiana University

[T]he recent push for educational choice, charters, and vouchers . . . is the strongest educational reform movement of the 1990s, and it is grounded entirely within the consumer-is-king perspective (Labaree, 1997, p. 38)

During the past two decades, a number of forces combined to encourage the privatization of the educational enterprise in the United States. Consumer-based control of education might be viewed as a natural next stage in the evolution of school governance, replacing professional control, which has prevailed throughout most of the twentieth century (Katz, 1992; Murphy, 1999). This chapter briefly explores the rationale for this movement, several of the most popular strategies to infuse market forces in public schooling, and implications of the movement to privatize education in the nation.

RATIONALE FOR PRIVATIZING GOVERNMENTAL SERVICES

Nationally, there is increasing sentiment that many governmental services should be privatized because of lack of confidence in public sector monopolies and concern that the government is controlling too much of our lives (Florestano, 1991; Lewis, 1993). Critics have lamented governmental inefficiencies that result in fiscal woes (Chubb & Moe, 1990; Richards, Shore, & Sawicky, 1966). Senge (1990) referred to business as the "locus of innovation in an open society" because it has "a freedom to experiment missing in the public sector and, often, in nonprofit organizations" (p. 15).

Many of the ideological and economic reasons offered for subjecting other governmental services to the marketplace are also used to support the privatization of education. Ideologically, there is increasing societal emphasis on encouraging entrepreneurial activity and individual advancement coupled with a renewed commitment to the free enterprise system. Doyle (1994) asserted that "the nation desperately needs new ways to conduct the business of educating the young, and entrepreneurship must be at the top of any list of reforms" (p. 129). The current focus on the consumer of education also is consistent with the notion of empowering parents and giving them more choice in determining the education of their children (Nathan, 1996). In addition, calls for privatizing schooling are grounded in the belief that problems associated with public schools simply cannot be remedied by the government. Critics claim that the years of overregulation of education by the government monopoly have provided few institutional incentives to move beyond the status quo (Buechler, 1996; Katz, 1992).

Economically, substantial business expansion in the information age will be in the service arena, so education is a likely target for corporate involvement (Murphy, 1999). Companies are eager to tap into the $310 billion spent annually on K–12 education in the United States (Schnaiberg, 1997; Vine, 1997). Also, many are doubting the efficacy of the state bureaucracy to deliver education in a postindustrial global economy (Lewis, 1993).

STRATEGIES TO INCREASE PRIVATE INVOLVEMENT IN EDUCATION

To place marketplace models to privatize education in the proper context, they must be viewed as comprising one strand among several efforts to improve education in our nation. For example, school improvement strategies being implemented *within* the public education enterprise range from standards-based reform and assessment (Buttram & Waters, 1997) to decentralization of education decisions to the school site (Keller, 1998; Patterson, 1998). Some strategies (e.g., magnet schools, alternative schools) are designed to provide options for parents and students, but these public school efforts to increase choice are not tied to market forces. In contrast, marketplace strategies reach beyond the confines of public school districts. Understanding these privatization efforts is important because they could have significant ramifications in changing the basic values and assumptions that guide schooling in the nation. This article focuses on implications of the most popular privatization strategies, specifically voucher systems, charter schools, and private management of schools.

Voucher Systems

In its basic form, a voucher system is a marketplace model that distributes governmental funds for education through vouchers of a specified amount that parents can redeem at public or *private* schools.[1] Various types of voucher proposals are being considered in a number of states, and a few limited voucher programs are being implemented. One of the main justifications for voucher programs is that private schools are assertedly of higher quality than public schools and the competitive environment will cause public schools to improve. Inferior schools will lose students and eventually go out of business through natural selection. Advocates of voucher systems further contend that a competitive environment will enhance the professional status and salaries of teachers and provide poor families with choices that only the rich have previously enjoyed. In addition, they assert that conversion to a marketplace model, with accountability focused on the school rather than the school district, will enhance student performance, parental involvement, and the efficient use of school funds (see Chubb & Moe, 1990; Nathan, 1989).

Many of the concerns over a marketplace model center around social justice and the impact of a voucher system on families who lack the interest or means to make informed choices (see Fowler, 1991; Rothstein & Rasell, 1993; Shanker & Rosenberg, 1991). Critics fear that a marketplace model will be the death knell for the common school with its democratizing function and will intensify economic and racial segregation (Goodlad, 1997). They argue that middle-class parents will desert public schools, leaving the disadvantaged and special-need students in public education. They also contend that voucher systems will unconstitutionally entangle the government with religious schools.

Teachers' unions have worked tirelessly at considerable expense to defeat voucher proposals in various states. Unions are well organized with sophisticated lobbying mechanisms, and they fear that gains made through collective bargaining are jeopardized by voucher plans and other privatization efforts. Any strategy that "threatens to displace existing workers, especially teachers, is going to be accused of union busting" (McLaughlin, 1995, p. 10).

Despite substantial discussion of voucher systems, the actual number of operational programs that include private schools is quite small. Several school districts in a few New England states have had de facto voucher systems for years; instead of operating their own high schools, they have provided tuition grants that high school students can use to attend public or private schools outside the district. But voucher initiatives have not fared well at the ballot box. Proposals that would have allowed state-supported vouchers to be redeemed at private schools were soundly defeated in Oregon in 1990, Colorado in 1992, California in 1993, and Washington in 1996. Indeed, since the 1960s, voters in 14 states have rejected state-supported voucher plans ("Get the Message Out," 1998).

Nonetheless, there has been renewed interest in voucher plans since the mid-1990s. In 1999, Florida became the first state to adopt a statewide voucher plan that includes religious schools (Sandham, 1999). Under the Florida program, students attending schools that are rated as deficient (based on test scores, attendance, graduation rates, and other factors) are entitled to state vouchers that can be used in qualified public or private schools of their choice. Also, a number of cities are experimenting with voucher plans for disadvantaged youth, under which parents can send their children to private schools through donation-supported vouchers. The Children's Educational Opportunity Foundation of America (CEO America), founded in 1991, currently distributes approximately $45 million across 31 voucher programs serving 12,000 students in major cities throughout the United States ("Supporters of Privately Financed Vouchers Tout Progress," 1998; Walsh, 1998b). Many of these programs follow the Golden Rule model, launched by Patrick Rooney of the Golden Rule Insurance Company in Indianapolis, under which scholarships typically cover about half of qualifying students' tuition up to a specified limit (e.g., $1,000). Theodore Forstmann, senior partner of a New York-based investment firm, and John Walton, son of the founder of WalMart, together have pledged $100 million for school vouchers, which they will make available to cities across the country where local sponsors are willing to provide matching funds (Archer, 1998b; Walsh, 1998b).

In San Antonio, which has had a privately funded voucher system since 1992, the CEO America announced in 1998 that it will provide $5 million annually for 10 years for students identified as at risk (free or reduced lunch) in the Edgewood School District to go to schools of their choice. Nearly all (93%) of the 14,000 students in this predominantly Hispanic school district qualify for the program, which makes this the first voucher program to provide a private school option for all low income children in a school district (Walsh, 1998b). This district was chosen because it was small enough for the Foundation to support every eligible child, and it was large enough for the scholarships to have an impact.

Several other foundations are financing more limited voucher efforts. For example, the Avi Chai Foundation has underwritten a voucher program to provide annual scholarships of $3,000 to elementary school children in Atlanta and Cleveland who will enroll in participating Jewish day schools ("Jewish Philanthropy to Test Vouchers," 1998). Parents who already enroll their children in these schools are not eligible to apply for these vouchers. The scholarships cover less than half of the tuition and are designed to entice more middle and upper middle income families to enroll their children in these schools.

In addition to these privately funded plans, voucher programs in Milwaukee and Cleveland are *publicly* funded. The Milwaukee choice program, initiated in 1990, provides vouchers for up to 1,500 low-income students to attend private, nonreligious schools. An attempt in 1995 to expand the program to include religious schools sparked considerable controversy. After the Wisconsin Supreme Court deadlocked on the constitutionality of the provision (*State v. Jackson*, 1996), a state appeals court struck down the program. The Wisconsin Supreme Court again reviewed the case in 1998, this time upholding the inclusion of private schools in the publicly funded voucher program (*Jackson v. Benson*, 1998).

The Cleveland program also provides vouchers that low-income parents can redeem in public or private schools, including religious schools. In 1999, the Ohio Supreme Court invalidated the program because it was attached to the state appropriations bill instead of enacted as a separate provision with its own allocation (*Simmons-Harris v. Goff*, 1999). This is a defect that the Ohio legislature can correct. Voucher advocates were encouraged that the state high court rejected the lower court's conclusion that the program provided direct and substantial governmental aid to sectarian schools in violation of the First Amendment's Establishment Clause. The Ohio Supreme Court was not persuaded that the program's primary effect was to benefit religious schools, even though no public schools participated in the scholarship program. After the Ohio legislature reinstated the voucher program in a law remedying the technical defect of the earlier provision, the measure was immediately challenged in federal court as abridging the Establishment Clause. The federal district court concluded that the program unconstitutionally advances religion, but the program remains operational for children already enrolled while an appeal is pending (*Simmons-Harris v. Zelman*, 1999). Until the legal status of voucher programs that include private schools is clarified by the Supreme Court, targeted programs will continue to be adopted, which in turn will generate litigation (see Archer, 1998a; "Pa. Voucher Plan Challenged," 1998).

Although assertions abound, there are too few voucher programs for much evaluation data to be available, and no hard evidence establishes that the limited voucher programs in operation result in student achievement gains (Ascher, Fruchter, & Berne,1996; Metcalf, 1997; Rothstein & Rasell, 1993). For example, student achievement data from the state-supported voucher programs in Milwaukee and Cleveland have been inconclusive, with studies to date reporting conflicting results (See Greene, Peterson, & Du, 1997; Metcalf, 1998; Rouse, 1998; Witte, 1998; Witte, Sterr, & Thorn, 1995). Similarly, the few privately funded programs offering scholarships for students to attend private schools have not yet provided evidence of significant gains in student performance (Martinez, Kemerer, & Goodwin, 1993; Weinschrott & Kilgore, 1996).

Despite the lack of conclusive evaluation data, some interesting demographic information has been gathered on families participating in the public choice program in Milwaukee and in several of the private programs. A 1993 study reported that Milwaukee families selecting private schools for their children were smaller; parents making this choice, especially mothers, were better educated with higher education expectations for their children and they worked at home more with their children on educational concerns (Witte, Bailey, & Thorne, 1993). Research studies on the Indianapolis and San Antonio privately funded choice programs similarly have documented that families who select private education differ from those who remain in public schools in that the former are more interested and involved in their children's education (Martinez, Thomas, & Kemerer, 1994; Weinschrott & Kilgore, 1996).

The final word on voucher systems using public funds may come from the courts. It has not yet been clarified whether voucher systems that allow public funds to be used for sectarian education could survive legal challenges under the Establishment Clause or similar provisions in state constitutions that prohibit the use of public funds for religious purposes. Several Supreme Court decisions lend support to the contention that state aid flowing to religious schools because of the *private choices* of parents would satisfy the Establishment Clause. As early as 1983, the Supreme Court recognized that a state's "decision to defray the cost of educational expenses incurred by parents—regardless of the type of schools their children attend—evidences a purpose that is both secular and understandable" (*Mueller v. Allen*, 1983, p. 395). Subsequently, the Court upheld the use of federal vocational rehabilitation aid for an individual to pursue preparation for the ministry (*Witters v. Washington Department*, 1986).

The Supreme Court has distinguished governmental aid that flows to religious schools through private choices of individuals from unconstitutional direct state aid to such schools. For example, in 1993, it found no Establishment Clause violation in using public funds to support a sign language interpreter for a hearing-impaired child attending a parochial school (*Zobrest v. Catalina Foothills School District*, 1993). In its most recent ruling related to this topic, *Agostini v. Felton* (1997), the Court upheld the use of public school personnel to provide remedial services in sectarian schools (under the Title I federal aid program for disadvantaged students), reasoning that this practice does not entail governmental support of religious schools. The Court noted that the remedial services are neutrally distributed to all eligible children irrespective of where they attend school. A voucher proposal that aids religious institutions because of *private* choices might also be viewed as religiously neutral legislation.

As discussed previously, the Wisconsin and Ohio high courts have rejected Establishment Clause challenges to the involvement of religious schools in voucher programs in Cleveland and Milwaukee, but the Cleveland plan remains in federal litigation and its legality is tenuous. In 1994, the Puerto Rico Supreme Court invalidated a program providing vouchers of $1,500 that low-income students could redeem in public or private schools as abridging the Puerto Rico constitutional ban on using public funds to support private education (*Associacion de Puerto Rico Maestros v. Torres*, 1994). More recently, the First Circuit Court of Appeals upheld Maine's program authorizing school districts without high schools to pay tuition for secondary students to attend public or nonsectarian private schools outside their districts, indicating that the program would run afoul of the Establishment Clause if it included religious schools (*Strout v. Albanese*, 1999). The Vermont Supreme Court reached a similar conclusion in rejecting payments for parochial school tuition based on the state constitution's prohibition against compelling citizens to support religious worship (*Chittenden v. Vermont*, 1999). These decisions could affect other New England communities that support high school tuition for students to attend private or public schools outside their home school districts.

Even if state-supported voucher plans are able to withstand constitutional scrutiny, they face a significant barrier in terms of the fiscal impact on the state. Almost 12 percent of all students are currently supported by their parents at private schools or home education programs; these students would be eligible for tax support under a voucher program. The fiscal consequences of conversion to vouchers may scuttle any widespread endorsement, a fate similarly suffered by proposed legislation to provide tax benefits for educational expenses incurred by parents. As discussed in the next section, economic concerns may be one reason that charter school legislation is more palatable to the electorate than voucher systems.

Charter Schools

Unlike states' reluctance to adopt voucher systems to fund education, most states have eagerly embraced charter school legislation during the past few years. In 1993, only two states—Minnesota and California—had passed charter school legislation. By 1999, charter school legislation had been passed in three fourths of the states ("Charters: Laws Passed," 1999). Under most of the laws, charter schools receive state aid, but operate outside the requirements of the traditional public education bureaucracy (Wohlstetter & Anderson, 1994). The intent is to give schools the flexibility to innovate in instructional programs by reducing operational constraints. Charter schools can be proposed by existing public or private schools or groups/companies starting new schools, and government relationships with charter schools vary across states. Usually, the charter can be renegotiated after a specified period, with continuation depending on assessments of student performance. In 1999 almost 1,800 charter schools were operating, and they served about 350,000 students (Brockett, 1998; Research, Policy, & Practice, 2000). Charter schools are accountable to their sponsors, most often the local or state board of education, but sponsors can be other agencies. Charter schools tend to be smaller than public schools, and to date most have been established at the elementary school level.

An interesting feature of charter schools is their "hybrid" nature in that they reflect features associated with both public and private schools (Buechler, 1996, p. 4). Like public schools, they use governmental funds, must accept all students who enroll, cannot promote religious beliefs, and are accountable to the public entity specified in the charter. Similar to private schools, they operate outside many state regulations, and they must attract students. They are directly answerable to consumers (i.e., parents and students), who can select other schools if dissatisfied. Some contend that charter schools capitalize on the strengths of both the private and public sectors, providing "an appropriate compromise between the current public education system, with little or no market accountability, and a voucher system with little or no accountability to the public at large" (Buechler, 1996, p. 3).

The charter school movement has clearly gained substantial momentum during the past few years. Pipho (1995) observed that charter schools seem to have taken on "the aura of a 'silver bullet'—a magical solution to a variety of problems" (p. 742). Politicians view charter schools as an inexpensive reform strategy because additional tax funds are not required. Critics, however, fear that public education will be undermined as the number of charter schools increases. They are concerned that charter school legislation will lead through the back door to vouchers, thus funneling public funds into private schools and jeopardizing the democratizing function of public education (Hoff, 1993; McCarthy, 1997; "State Legislators," 1993).

Among national organizations now involved in the charter school movement is the National Education Association (NEA), which operates five charter schools. According to union officials, the organization wants to play a role in shaping the nature of charter schools nationally. It is not surprising that the NEA guidelines call for their charter schools to hire certified teachers and ensure that their working conditions are equal to those of teachers in other schools. Nonetheless, NEA's involvement has been controversial, with skepticism from some local NEA affiliates who have vigorously opposed legislation authorizing charter schools. There is some sentiment that charters in general threaten several basic beliefs of unions, such as ensuring similar status and treatment for all teachers (see Schnaiberg, 1998a). Nathan (1996), however, claimed that charter schools represent empowerment for teachers, rather than a threat, and that "the spirit behind the charter school movement [is] a deep respect for innovative educators" (p. 23).

Various types of unique charter schools are being established. For example, a charter in Raleigh, North Carolina serves youths awaiting adjudication in jail, and a residential charter in Minnesota is for court-placed delinquent youths. In Anchorage, Alaska, a charter school is intended for professional sports hopefuls. A few charters are designed to draw students from Religious Right families who were formerly home schooled; while the instructional programs are sensitive to the beliefs of these families, they do not include sectarian instruction (Brockett, 1998). In 1998, Milwaukee took the first steps toward sponsoring a charter school independent of the school district, becoming the first municipality to do so (Schnaiberg, 1998c).

Some charter schools are connected in various ways to the work environment. For example, worksite charter schools are designed to make it easier for working parents to get their children to school and to spend time with their children during the school day (Schnaiberg, 1998b). These schools are redefining the school community to encompass those who work in a given locale (e.g., medical center). One hurdle in establishing such workplace charters is that giving preference to workers of a particular employer is precluded under existing charter school legislation in many states. Other charter schools are being established to prepare students for particular jobs rather than to accommodate their parents' place of employment. For example, the Center for Appropriate Transport in Eugene, Oregon emphasizes preparing students for bicycle manufacturing, given that there are several bicycle factories in the surrounding area. Also, the Academy for Plastics Manufacturing Technology, a high school open to students from seven school districts in Michigan, was initially established because of the plastic firms' need for employees (Brockett, 1998).

Some groups, realizing how difficult it is to operate a charter school, are turning to for-profit companies to manage their schools. Murphy (1999) referred to private management as the second wave of the charter school movement. In 1997 about a dozen companies were operating approximately 10 percent of the charter schools nationally (Schnaiberg, 1997). Usually, the for-profit group does not hold the charter but contracts with local nonprofit partners. As discussed in the next section, critics of private management of public schools are concerned that profit motives will overshadow educational goals.

Serious evaluation data on charter schools are just beginning to be gathered (see Research, Policy, & Practice, 1999). Shavelson observed that although charter schools are appealing to the public, "the real issue is whether what goes on in the classroom has substantially changed" (quoted in Jacobson, 1996, p. 21). Do they do a better job of educating students and do they reinvigorate public schools by "injecting a strong dose of competition into the entire system?" (p. 21). Accountability is a difficult issue because consensus has not been reached regarding how the success of charter schools should be assessed. Should the schools be measured by traditional accountability systems (e.g., student performance on standardized tests), even though these schools are designed to be nontraditional (Schnaiberg, 1998d)? What role should parent satisfaction play in accountability systems? Other questions also need to be addressed, such as how does the racial and ethnic composition of students in charter schools compare with the student composition of other public schools? When there were only a handful of charters nationally, perhaps these questions did not seem as pressing as they do now that the number of charter schools is expanding rapidly.

Private Contractors

Current efforts of private companies to manage public schools and school districts have been extremely controversial. The developments pertaining to Educational Alternatives Incorporated (EAI) in Minneapolis have been illustrative.[2] After contracting to run single schools in a few districts, EAI signed a contract to manage nine Baltimore schools, but the project was plagued by disputes from the beginning. The teachers' union was a severe critic of EAI, challenging, among other things, that the company's decisions to increase class size and to replace teachers' aides from the community with student-teacher interns. It was reported that the cost of education in EAI schools was 7 to 11 percent higher than costs in other Baltimore elementary schools (Williams & Leak, 1996). Also, city officials in Baltimore called for an investigation of EAI after student achievement gains were overstated in the press in 1993, and the company had problems with the Maryland department of education over instructional programs for children with disabilities ("EAI Overstates," 1994). In 1995, with relations between school district and city officials and EAI becoming increasingly strained, the Baltimore school board terminated the EAI contract. Ironically, the previous spring's test results, released shortly after the contract cancellation, showed larger student achievement gains in the EAI-managed schools (Green, 1997).

In 1994, EAI signed a contract to manage 32 schools in Hartford, Connecticut, the largest contract awarded by a school district to date. This ambitious experiment, however, was aborted before it got off the ground. Amid opposition from the teachers' union and some local residents the project was scaled back, but relations became increasingly tense over how much money EAI was entitled to receive. Finally, in 1996 the school board voted to terminate the contract (Walsh, 1996). The company subsequently changed its name to Tesseract Group and moved its headquarters to Arizona. Although still involved in some school districts on a limited basis, its stock value has dropped significantly.

Another corporate effort to manage public schools, the Edison Project, was conceptualized by entrepreneur Chris Whittle who originally envisioned a national chain of private schools. For economic reasons the focus shifted to managing public schools, however, especially charter schools. Edison schools are intended to be radically different from traditional schools (e.g., multi-age grouping, differentiated staffing, longer school day and year, curriculum centered on great works). One claim is that computers will be in every student's home and on every teacher's desk in Edison schools. The typical school day is 8 hours long, and the school year is about 25 days longer than the standard public school calendar. The Edison Project spent an estimated $40 million in development before opening its first school (Walsh, 1998c).

Unlike EAI's initial plan to run entire school districts, Edison is not trying to take over all school district operations but, rather, to give parents a choice between educational philosophies within the district. The first four Edison schools began operating in the fall of 1995 ("Edison Project Reports Success," 1996), and by 1998, the Edison Project operated 25 elementary or middle schools in Boston; Colorado Springs; Mt. Clemens, Michigan; Sherman, Texas; Wichita, Kansas; Worcester, Massachusetts; Lansing, Michigan; Dade County, Florida; Chula Vista, California; Detroit, Duluth, and Flint, Michigan; and a small school district on the outskirts of San Antonio. By the end of 1999, Edison was operating 79 schools serving about 38,000 students (Walsh, 1999).

Edison released a report in December, 1997, indicating that students in its schools that opened in 1995 are experiencing notable achievement gains in reading and mathematics compared with control groups. The Wichita elementary school appears to be the most successful of Edison schools to date. The report also indicated that some scores across the four schools fell slightly for a few grade levels with no discernable patterns as to gains and losses (Walsh, 1998a). Other accounts of student progress in Edison schools have not been as positive as the company's own reports. For example, data on the Renaissance charter school in Boston have been mixed; there was almost 40 percent faculty turnover after its first year of operation

(Farber, 1998). Also, in 1998 the American Federation of Teachers (AFT) released a report critical of student achievement in Edison schools (AFT, 1998). The report reflected inconclusive results regarding whether students in Edison schools were doing as well as other students and questioned some of Edison's claims regarding student achievement gains and its implementation of special programs.

In addition to Edison and EAI, which have received most of the national publicity, numerous other private companies have become involved in public education with contracts based on promises of improved student performance. For example, Nashville's Alternative Public Schools, Inc. (APS) contracted to manage a school in Wilkinsburg, Pennsylvania. The teachers' union challenged the company's activities from the beginning, which slowed some of its initiatives. After a couple of rocky years, a state court ruled in 1997 that the school district lacked legal authority under state law to contract with APS to run the elementary school (Walsh, 1997).

The Minneapolis school board received considerable publicity in 1993 when it hired a local management consulting firm, Public Strategies Group (PSG), to run its schools, with the PSG president serving as superintendent ("Private Firm," 1993). PSG came into the contract with broad support in the community, and the school district adopted an improvement agenda for 1994 to 1995 that tied over $400,000 in incentive pay to PSG for achieving various performance objectives (Graves, 1995). The Minneapolis experiment ended June 30, 1997 on amiable terms, although the contract was supposed to run until August of 1998. The company indicated that it had accomplished what it set out to do, and the school board praised the accomplishments of PSG.

Other companies are seeking contracts to provide targeted instructional services. Sylvan Learning Systems, which has 500 private tutoring centers nationwide, has contracts in Baltimore, Chicago, Washington, DC, and a number of other school districts to provide remedial services (Walsh, 1995; 1996). Sylvan promises to measurably improve every participating student's reading and math skills within 12 months. Unlike EAI and the Edison Project, Sylvan has attracted little media attention, and teachers' unions do not see the company as a significant threat. It is not making school budgetary decisions; it is simply being paid to provide instructional services that formerly were provided by the school district. Other companies offering intensive tutoring or specialized instruction include Huntington Learning Centers, Britannica Learning Centers, Kaplan Educational Centers, Berlitz Language Schools, Ombudsman Educational Services, Futurekids, and Kumon Educational Institute (McLaughlin, 1992; "Private Firms," 1995).

These companies seeking limited contracts to provide targeted services face fewer obstacles than do companies trying to manage schools and districts. Corporations seem to have learned how difficult running schools can be, so more limited (and less controversial) involvement has appeal to the business world. Sylvan and similar companies are significantly increasing their involvement in public education. School boards are becoming more receptive to the idea that they do not have to provide all instructional services themselves as long as they ensure that the private vendors are doing a good job. Additional companies may decide that targeted instructional services hold the greatest economic promise for tapping the lucrative education market in the near future.

The use of private contractors to provide some services is appealing to school boards primarily for economic reasons. Financially strapped school districts under pressure to improve student learning often feel that they have little to risk with a company that will guarantee results; payment is contingent on students attaining certain performance standards. But critics fear that the corporate concern for realizing profits may result in short cuts that reduce the quality of educational services.

IMPLICATIONS

Schools mirror society; they do not drive it (Goodlad, 1997, p. 56)

Historically, the system of free public education in our nation has reflected the American citizenry's recognition of the importance of education in a democracy. The Supreme Court has recognized that education ranks at the very apex of the functions of a state (*Wisconsin v. Yoder*, 1972, p. 213), and traditionally a central purpose of public schooling has been to inculcate citizenship values in the next generation. But concerns are being raised that these public interests are being subjugated to individual interests in personal advancement. Labaree (1997) observed that traditionally there have been periodic shifts in emphasis between two goals for education, democratic equality and social efficiency, but that there has been steady growth throughout the twentieth century in the influence a third goal—social mobility—which has become a dominant force in American education. Both the equity and efficiency goals treat education as a public good that benefits all members of the community, but the social mobility goal is quite different as it focuses on the individual consumer (rather than the citizen or taxpayer) and treats education as a private good. Most of the options to increase private investment in education, such as unregulated voucher plans, favor the individual's advancement over collective concerns, with schools primarily accountable to the consumer. Labaree questions "who will look after the public's interest in education" in a consumer-oriented educational system (p. 38).

Although different assumptions guide the various options to privatize education, there are some values that undergird most of the strategies to inject market forces in public education. For example, voucher systems, private management of school districts, and private contracting for limited services all place high value on productivity and efficiency. Usually, efficiency is measured in terms of increased student learning and lower costs. Private companies that are attempting to contract with school districts usually assert that they can produce more learning for less money, which is quite enticing to school officials. Skeptics of private contracting, however, assert that the educational goal of producing a better society will be subjugated to attaining higher test scores in the name of increasing school efficiency (Houston, 1994). The bottom line for private companies is to please stockholders in terms of profits, whereas public school districts must serve the entire society (Spillane & Regnier, 1998).

Voucher systems and charter schools, as well as some corporate involvement in education, also emphasize empowering parents so that they can make educational choices in line with their personal beliefs and values. One of the few conclusive findings from the studies of voucher programs operating to date is that parents are more satisfied and involved with the schools that they have been allowed to select for their children (Martinez, Thomas, & Kemerer, 1994; Weinschrott & Kilgore, 1996). Those advocating marketplace models of schooling want parents, rather than educators or policy makers, to be the primary architects of their children's education. Instead of state-prescribed values being advanced in public schools, parents would select the educational setting that reinforces their own beliefs. They favor control by lay citizens over control by educational professionals (Murphy, 1999).

A related assumption implicitly undergirding many privatization models is that homogeneity within individual schools should take precedence over diversity. Under marketplace models, social homogeneity is considered important to a school's performance because it reduces conflict about goals; each school need attract only a small slice of the market (Chubb & Moe, 1990). As noted previously, Edison Project officials want parents to have a choice so that those selecting an Edison school believe in the school's philosophy (McGriff, 1995).

Another related assumption is that governmental control of education needs to be reduced because it has led to bureaucratized, ineffective schools (Chubb & Moe, 1990; Doyle, 1994). Advocates of vouchers desire local school autonomy and accountability, and a central feature of most charter school legislation is that state controls are relaxed for the schools awarded charters. One reason charter school legislation appeals to Edison Project officials is that their design cannot be implemented under restrictive governmental regulations.

Reduced governmental control in education raises significant questions about the state's oversight role in protecting individual rights and guaranteeing that all children receive an education necessary for citizenship in a democracy. The President's Commission on Privatization (1988) cautioned that where public institutions have assumed important democratic functions, the shift toward market alternatives may jeopardize core values of our society. As noted previously, some fear that increased privatization will lead to the demise of democratic control of education (Goodlad, 1997).

In carrying out its responsibility to protect the citizenry, must the state ensure that all children are exposed to certain values and academic content to advance the common good (McCarthy, 1997)? Or should parents, with minimal governmental constraints, be able to dictate the content of their children's education and the values to which they are exposed? Are there limits on how far we can go in privatizing education without jeopardizing the form of government we have adopted in our nation? If an individual school—public or private—is allowed to determine its curriculum with little oversight, might the state be abdicating its responsibility to protect children and to ensure an educated citizenry? Should all proposals to privatize education be required to satisfy a series of criteria (e.g., to improve rather than exacerbate social ills, to promote cultural unity rather than increase divisions, to reduce inequities in education and not aggravate them, to help all people become economically self-sufficient) (Center on National Education Policy, 1996; Pipho, 1998)? These are important questions that require thoughtful attention.

CONCLUSION

The school privatization movement has resulted in a number of ideological clashes (McCarthy, 1997). Bauman (1996) observed that social market theory entails a "reduced role for government, greater consumer control, and a belief in efficiency and individuality over equity and community" (p. 627). Some argue that the emphasis on individual advancement over the collective good is positive for our national commitment to free enterprise and an entrepreneurial spirit (Doyle, 1994). Others assert that an emphasis on consumerism in education will be devastating for our nation and that the needs of children will become secondary to economic motives (Rist, 1991). Goodlad (1997) asserted that the philosophical shift toward privatization of public services "is evidence that even the political democracy we have striven so hard to attain is adrift from its moral moorings" (p. 56).

The past decade has witnessed a steady increase in private investment in education, far surpassing private involvement in public schooling at any other time in the history of our nation (Spillane & Regnier, 1998). In 1996, the first Annual Education Industry Conference was held in New York City and drew several hundred potential investors and education leaders (Doyle, 1996). There is particular political receptivity to charter schools and to programs under which companies contract to provide intensive tutoring or instruction in technology in public schools. Companies, school boards, consumers, and the general citizenry all have a stake in the direction that efforts to privatize education take in our nation and should heed lessons learned from experiences to date. Also, policy makers need to understand the values undergirding various models of corporate involvement in education so that informed decisions can be made.

If the movement toward privatization means that the purposes and basic structure of public education in our nation are being fundamentally changed, then policy makers need to explore fully the implications of this shift for children, parents, corporations, and the general public. If we are no longer concerned about what education "can do for democracy or the economy but what it can do for me" (Labaree, 1997, p. 38), we should at least recognize the ramifications of this ideological change, because they reach beyond public schooling. Unless we are attentive, we may by default embrace policies that are inconsistent with democratic principles, which many Americans are not ready to abandon.

NOTES

1. Parts of this chapter build on "Privatization of education: Friendly or hostile takeover" (McCarthy, 1997).

2. Another aspect of private involvement in public education receiving increasing attention pertains to use of public schools for commercial activities, most notably advertising. Chris Whittle gained national prominence when he launched Channel One, a 10-minute news program with advertisements. In return for guaranteeing that students watch the program, schools receive free equipment, and about 12,000 schools currently use Channel One. Numerous other efforts to inject advertising in public schools are gaining popularity. For example, the largest school district in Colorado (Jefferson County) signed a contract in 1997 under which Pepsi is donating $2.1 million to help build a new football stadium in return for the right to advertise its products in the district's stadiums, fields, and gymnasiums and for the exclusive right to sell soft drinks in all 140 school buildings (Pipho, 1997).

REFERENCES

Agostini v. Felton, 521 U.S. 203 (1997).

American Federation of Teachers. (1998). *Student achievement in Edison schools: Mixed results in an ongoing enterprise.* Washington, DC: AFT.

American Federation of Teachers. (1994). *The private management of public schools: An analysis of the EAI experience in Baltimore.* Washington, DC: AFT.

Archer, J. (1998a, April 1). Pa. District gives go ahead to local voucher plan. *Education Week,* 3.

Archer, J. (1998b, June 10). Millionaires to back national voucher project. *Education Week,* 3.

Ascher, C., Fruchter, N., & Berne, R. (1996). *Hard lessons: Public schools and privatization.* New York: Twentieth Century Fund Press.

Associacion de Puerto Rico Maestros v. Torres, No. 94-371, 1994 WL 780744 (Puerto Rico, 1994).

Bauman, P. C. (1996, November). Governing education in an antigovernment environment. *Journal of School Leadership, 6,* 625–643.

Brockett, D. (1998, May 12). Charter laws pave the way for unusual schools. *School Board News,* 1, 12.

Buechler, M. (1996). *Charter schools: Legislation and results after four years* (PR-B13). Bloomington: Indiana Education Policy Center.

Buttram, J. L., & Waters, T. (1997). Improving America's schools through standards-based education. *NASSP Bulletin, 81* (590), 1–6.

Center on National Education Policy. (1996). *Do we still need public schools?* Bloomington, IN: Phi Delta Kappa.

Charters: Laws passed as unionization plan defeated. (1999, June 11). *School Law News,* 4.

Chittenden Town School District v. Vermont Department of Education, 38 A.2d 539 (Vt. 1999), cert. denied, 120 S. Ct. 626 (1999).

Chubb, J. E., & Moe, T. M. (1990). *Politics, markets, and America's schools.* Washington, DC: Brookings Institute.

Doyle, D. (1994). The role of private sector management in public education. *Phi Delta Kappan, 76,* 128–132.

Doyle, D. (1996, March 20). Education supply: Will it create demand? *Education Week, 37,* 48.

EAI overstates student progress in its schools. (1994, June 21). *School Board News,* 7.

Edison project reports success. (1996, December 24). *School Board News,* 1, 9.

Farber, P. (1998). The Edison Project scores—and stumbles—in Boston. *Phi Delta Kappan, 79,* 506–512.

Florestano, P. S. (1991). Considerations for the future. In R. L. Kemp (Ed.), *Privatization: The provision of public services by the private sector* (pp. 291–296). Jefferson, NC: McFarland.

Fowler, F. C. (1991). The shocking ideological integrity of Chubb and Moe. *Journal of Education, 173,* 119–129.

Get the message out: Vouchers will weaken public education. (1998, February 10). *School Board News,* 4.

Goodlad, J. (1997, July 9). Making democracy safe for education. *Education Week,* 40, 56.

Graves, P. (1995). Putting pay on the line. *The School Administrator, 52*(2), 8–15.

Green, P. C. (1997). To a peaceful settlement: Using constructive methods to terminate contracts between private corporations and school districts. *Equity & Excellence in Education, 30*(2), 39–48.

Greene, J., Peterson, P., & Du, J. (1997, March). *The effectiveness of school choice: The Milwaukee experiment* (Harvard University Education Policy and Governance Occasional Paper no. 97-1). Cambridge: Harvard University.

Hoff, D. (1993, June 4). State legislators embrace charter schools over choice. *Education Daily, 1,* 3.

Houston, P. (1994). Making watches or making music. *Phi Delta Kappan, 76,* 133–135.

Jackson v. Benson, 570 N.W.2d 407 (Wis. App. 1997), rev'd, 578 N.W.2d 602 (1998), cert. denied, 119 S. Ct. 466 (1998).

Jacobson, L. (1996, November 6). Under the microscope. *Education Week,* 21–23.

Jewish philanthropy to test vouchers in Jewish schools in Atlanta, Cleveland. (1998, April 22). *Education Week,* 6.

Katz, M. B. (1992). Chicago school reform as history. *Teachers College Record, 94*(1), 56–72.

Keller, B. (1998, May 6). Report calls for decentralization of Detroit school administration, *Education Week,* 12.

Labaree, D. F. (1997, September 17). Are students "consumers"? The rise of public education as a private good. *Education Week,* 38, 48.

Lewis, D. A. (1993). Deinstitutionalization and school decentralization: Making the same mistake twice. In J. Hannaway & M. Carnoy (Eds.), *Decentralization and school improvement* (pp. 84–101). San Francisco: Jossey-Bass.

Martinez, V., Kemerer, F., & Goodwin, K. (1993). *Who chooses and why?* Denton, TX: University of North Texas.

Martinez, V., Thomas, K., & Kemerer, F. (1994). Who chooses and why: A look at five school district choice plans. *Phi Delta Kappan, 75,* 678–681.

McCarthy, M. (1997). School privatization: Friendly or hostile takeover? In M. McClure & J. Lindle (Eds.), *Expertise versus responsiveness in children's worlds* (pp. 61–69). London: Falmer Press.

McGriff, D. (1995). Lighting the way for systemic reform. *The School Administrator, 52*(7), 14–19.

McLaughlin, J. (1992). Schooling for profit: Capitalism's new frontier. *Educational Horizons, 71,* 23–30.

McLaughlin, J. (1995). Public education and private enterprise. *The School Administrator, 52*(7), 7–12.

Metcalf, K. (1997). *A comparative evaluation of the Cleveland scholarship and tutoring grant program.* Bloomington: The Indiana Center for Evaluation.

Metcalf, K. (1998). *Evaluation of the Cleveland scholarship program: Second-year report (1997–98).* Bloomington: The Indiana Center for Evaluation.

Mueller v. Allen, 463 U.S. 388 (1983).

Murphy, J. (1999). New consumerism: Evolving market dynamics in the institutional dimension of schooling. In J. Murphy & K. Seashore-Lewis (Eds.), *The handbook of research on educational administration* (2nd ed., pp. 405–419). San Francisco: Jossey-Bass.

Nathan, J. (1989). Progress, problems and prospects with state choice plans. In J. Nathan (Ed.), *Public schools by choice* (pp. 203–224). St. Paul, MN: The Institute for Learning and Teaching.

Nathan, J. (1996). Possibilities, problems, and progress. *Phi Delta Kappan, 78,* 18–24.

Pa. voucher plan challenged. (1998, April 22). *Education Week,* 4.

Patterson, J. (1998). Harsh realities about decentralized decision making. *The School Administrator, 55*(3), 6–12.

Pipho, C. (1995). The expected and the unexpected. *Phi Delta Kappan, 76,* 742–743.

Pipho, C. (1997). The selling of public education. *Phi Delta Kappan, 79,* 101–102.

Private firms in the school marketplace. (1995). *The School Administrator, 52*(7), 8.

Private firm will run Minneapolis schools. (1993, November 23). *School Board News,* 1, 6.

President's Commission on Privatization. (1988). *Privatization: Toward more effective government.* Washington, DC: United States Government Printing Office.

Research, Policy, & Practice, Int. & Center for Applied Research and Educational Improvement. (2000). *National study of charter schools: Fourth-year report.* Washington, DC: United States Department of Education.

Richards, C. E., Shore, R., & Sawicky, M. B. (1996). *Risky business: Private management of public schools.* Washington, DC: Economic Policy Institute.

Rist, M. C. (1991). Whittling away at public education. *The Executive Educator, 13*(9), 22–28.

Rothstein, R., & Rasell, E. (Eds.) (1993). *School choice: Examining the evidence.* Arlington, VA: Public Interest Publications.

Rouse, C. E. (1998). Schools and student achievement: More evidence from the Milwaukee parental choice program. *Economic Policy Review, 4,* 61–76.

Sandham, J. (1999, May 5). Florida OKs first statewide voucher plan. *Education Week,* 1, 21.

Schnaiberg, L. (1997, December 10). Firms hoping to turn profit from charters. *Education Week*, 1, 14.

Schnaiberg, L. (1998a, March 11). In midst of skepticism and scrutiny, NEA's 5 charter schools push on. *Education Week*, 1, 14.

Schnaiberg, L. (1998b, March 25). Worksite charter schools take the edge off commuting. *Education Week*, 8–9.

Schnaiberg, L. (1998c, April 29). Milwaukee may adopt its own charter plan. *Education Week*, 10.

Schnaiberg, L. (1998d, June 10). Charter schools struggle with accountability. *Education Week*, 1, 14.

Senge, P. M. (1990). *The fifth discipline*. New York: Doubleday.

Shanker, A., & Rosenberg, B. (1991, Winter). *Politics, markets, and schools: The fallacies of private school choice*. Washington, DC: American Federation of Teachers.

Spillane, R., & Regnier, P. (1998). A world apart: Decision making in the public and private sectors. *The School Administrator, 55*(3), 20–22.

State legislators embrace charter schools over choice. (1993, June 4). *Education Daily*, 1, 3.

State v. Jackson, 546 N.W.2d 140 (Wis. 1996).

Simmons-Harris v. Goff, 684 N.E.2d 705 (Ohio App. 1997), *rev'd*, 711 N.E.2d 203 (Ohio 1999).

Simmons-Harris v. Zelman, 54 F.Supp.2d 725 (N.D. Ohio, 1999).

Strout v. Albanese, 178 F.3d 57 (1st Cir. 1999), cert. denied, 120 S.Ct. 329 (1999).

Supporters of privately financed vouchers tout progress. (1998, May 6). *Education Week*, 14.

Vine, P. (1997). To market, to market . . . the school business sells kids short. *Nation, 265* (7), 11–16.

Walsh, M. (1995, November 29). Sylvan makes quiet inroads into public schools. *Education Week*, 3, 12.

Walsh, M. (1996, February 21). Brokers pitch education as hot investment. *Education Week*, 1, 15.

Walsh, M. (1997, September 3). Judge's ruling could end school-privatization venture. *Education Week*, 15.

Walsh, M. (1998a, January 14). Edison project prepares to expand, thanks to new private investment. *Education Week*, 7.

Walsh, M. (1998b, April 29). Group offers $50 million for vouchers. *Education Week*, 1, 22.

Walsh, M. (1998c, May 27). Edison schools predict "watershed year" ahead. *Education Week*, 5.

Walsh, M. (1999, December 15). Report card on for-profit industry still incomplete. *Education Week*, 14–16.

Weinschrott, D. J., & Kilgore, S. B. (1996). *Educational Choice Charitable Trust: An experiment in school choice*. Indianapolis: Hudson Institute.

Williams, L. C., & Leak, L. E. (1996). School privatization's first big test: EAI in Baltimore. *Educational Leadership, 54*(2), 56–60.

Wisconsin v. Yoder, 406 U.S. 205 (1972).

Witte, J. (1998). The Milwaukee voucher experiment. *Education Evaluation and Policy Analysis, 20*, 229–251.

Witte, J., Bailey, A., & Thorn, C. (1993). *Third-year report: Milwaukee parental choice program*. Madison: University of Wisconsin-Madison.

Witte, J., Sterr, T., & Thorn, C. (1995). *Fifth-year report: Milwaukee parental choice program*. Madison: University of Wisconsin-Madison.

Witters v. Washington Department of Services for the Blind, 474 U.S. 481 (1986).

Wohlstetter, P., & Anderson, L. (1994). What can U.S. charter schools learn from England's grant-maintained schools? *Phi Delta Kappan, 75*, 486–491.

Zobrest v. Catalina Foothills School District, 509 U.S. 1 (1993).

3

TRANSACTION COSTS AND THE STRUCTURE OF INTERAGENCY COLLABORATIVES: BRIDGING THEORY AND PRACTICE

Patrick Galvin and Janice Fauske
University of Utah

INTRODUCTION

Restructuring educational organizations involves alterations in patterns of rules, roles, relationships, goals, and expectations. New rules governing decision making and the behavior of educational leaders are manifest in the pervasive trend toward shared governance structures described as site-based management, partnerships, and similar collaborative efforts. These efforts at restructuring are associated with changes in how we think about organizations. If once we viewed organizations as closed systems where authority and decision-making power were fixed in a determined hierarchy, today we see them as a open systems based on collaborative networks[1] both within and between organizations. It is the dissolution of organizational boundaries that characterizes these changes in organizational theory. In this respect, organizations are increasingly viewed as a set of horizontal relationships more like a web than a strictly defined hierarchy of power relations.

This emerging view of organizations and governance has had a significant influence on policy makers, especially in the social service area. It is widely asserted that the problems of today's society and youth are too complex for any one agency to address alone (Mattessich & Monsey, 1992). Where collaborative services can be coordinated, professionals can "create an envelop of support" for families and children that overcomes a debilitating effect of service fragmentation and redundancy (Lawson, 1995). In this perspective, collaboration is described as an essential element to good and successful social policy (Melaville & Blank, 1993).

Although collaboration among organizations has rapidly expanded during the 1980s and 1990s, evidence suggests that many are short-lived and end with high levels of dissatisfaction among participants (both in the public and private sector). For example, Kusserow (1991) reviewed 20 years of effort to promote integration among social service agencies and concluded that most failed to change the structure and operation of the participating organizations in any substantial way. The promise of collaboration is equally fraught with problems in the business community; the literature describing for-profit collaborative estimates that as many as 70 percent fail to meet their performance expectations (Pearce, 1997). Why does such a potentially good idea appear to fail so frequently? Considering why so many collaboratives fail leads to another critical question: why do some collaboratives succeed? This study pursues these questions.

Our investigation of eight large inter-agency collaborations, collective efforts involving schools and social service agencies from around the country, reveals a surprising finding. These collaboratives, which were designed to share resources and expertise through the creation of horizontal relationships, have formed small-scale, top-down management structures to govern their collaborative work. We call these governance structures "intermediate hierarchies" because they regulate rules and expectations in a bridging fashion between otherwise independent organizations.

The purpose of this chapter is to describe problems that undermine collaborative efforts and explain how intermediate hierarchies help resolve those problems. The framework for discussion of these matters draws from a field of inquiry known as transaction cost theory. The ideas underlying this theory, which are founded by Coase (1937) and pioneered by Oliver Williamson during the 1970s (Williamson, 1975; Williamson & Masten, 1995), provide a rich framework for identifying the risks and costs associated with collaborative governance and the reasons why hierarchical structures help to relieve these costs. Against this backdrop of theory, we examine the reality of the previously mentioned eight collaborative efforts. The chapter concludes with a summary of the conditions that support and sustain collaboration. In this respect, we hope that the information serves to bridge the theory–practice gap surrounding the conceptualization versus implementation of collaborative interorganizational structures.

POLICY AND PRACTICE: THEORY AND REALITY

The presentation of this chapter is partly organized around the tension between policy makers, as the conceptualizers of collaboration, and practitioners, as the implementers of collaboration. Policy makers typically prescribe solutions to practitioners through the discussion and passage of legislation promoting policy goals. Policy makers must attempt to clearly define the nature of problems and their solutions within the context of legislation and politics. By contrast, practitioners work in the particulars of programs and people and are grounded in their field of practice, where problems and solutions are perpetually in a state of exploration and negotiation. The implementation of policy into practice is the gray area between policy makers and practitioners (First, 1996). Policy makers envision broad solutions to problems through legislation and policies, but practitioners do not always implement policies in ways consistent with the intent of policy makers. In many ways, this disparity can be characterized in terms of inductive and deductive views of a problem.

This distinction between deductive and inductive views reflects a similar tension between the research approaches of the authors. Research can be described as either deductive or inductive. Deductive research attempts to test hypotheses derived from existing theories. By contrast, researchers who apply inductive research design attempt to describe reality as it is, exploring the complexity of the phenomenon of interest bit by bit. The deductive framework, we believe, is like that used by policy makers; the policy makers derive policies (hypotheses) from existing theories that describe how they believe the system works. The inductive framework is like that of the practitioners; practitioners build an operative theory of collaboration from the synthesis of their experience.[2]

In this discussion, the authors rely on both the deductive and inductive frameworks to make sense of collaboration. Descriptions of practice are, thus, "juxtaposed" with descriptions of theory in an effort to explain the organization of collaboratives. The purpose is to use theory to make sense of the dynamic reality we call policy and practice rather than to test or build theory. We draw strength from these two methodological approaches in an effort to clarify problems that undermine otherwise promising policies and practices related to collaboration.

These parallels in theory and practice lead us to the organization of the next few sections of the chapter, where we alternately compare the assumptions and theories of policy makers and then practitioners of collaboration. First, we show how differently these two groups of actors think about collaboration, although they are pursuing similar ends. Second, these working theories help ground the discussion of transaction cost theories of collaboration and organization that follows.

ASSUMPTIONS OF POLICY MAKERS ABOUT COLLABORATION

Around the country, numerous interagency collaboratives have been formed. In Connecticut, the state Department of Education has funded 18 programs, which are collectively known as Family Resource Centers (Plant & King, 1995). Other states like Kentucky and Minnesota, as well as cities like Chicago and San Francisco, have developed programs aimed at coordinating the resources and activities of educational and human service agencies (Ryan, Adams, Gullotta, Weissberg, & Hampton, 1995). Indeed, the idea of collaboration is widely cited as an essential ingredient to successful reform, a point the Office of Educational Research and Improvement made explicit in its call for education and social service reforms (Klein, Medrich, & Perez-Ferreiro, 1996). In all these cases, the underlying argument for interagency collaboration is that schools and other service agencies can not adequately address the complex problems confronting families and communities (Melaville & Blank, 1993).

The rationale for collaboration is founded on three sets of ideas. First, there is pressing evidence that the problems facing parents and families profoundly affect the capacity of schools to educate children. Children who arrive at school hungry, abused, or neglected are not ready to learn. Thus, it is not surprising the readiness to learn is one of the Goals 2000 and the National Governor's Association (Association, 1990) objectives. Second, the current organization of social services is not well suited to deal with the complex problems facing families and communities. For the most part, social service agencies are crisis oriented and their services are fragmented among different agencies (Lawson, 1995). Third, there is a widespread belief that enlisting the support of parents, community members, professionals, and business representatives will create an environment in which schools can be restructured (Crowson & Morris, 1985; Melaville & Blank, 1993; Ryan et al., 1995)

With this evidence that considerable policy supports the promotion of collaboratives among policy makers, we turn to the assumptions underlying these efforts. There is no definitive line between the policy maker and practitioner, we envision the policy makers as those individuals responsible for the development, passage, and administration of policies governing practice. We assume that they conduct their business with some theoretical orientation, and that policy formulation is guided by more than reactions based on self-interest. When we think through the ideas that underlie the general propositions stated, six key factors appear to shape the values and beliefs that represent a policy maker's theory of collaboration.

- Policy makers assume that people who are required to collaborate have the skills to do so and understand the process.
- Policy makers assume that collaboration, working together, is desirable, particularly with regard to education and social services.
- Policy makers assume that collaboration can be implemented by laws, policies, political exchange, or creating administrative structures.
- Policy makers assume that professionals within organizations can transcend their agendas to address shared objectives and discount issues of territoriality and protection of resources.
- Policy makers assume an economy of scale with collaboration across subunits of government such as social services, law enforcement, and school districts.

- Policy makers and practitioners discuss collaboration in terms of examples rather than concepts or theories.

Two assumptions seem especially significant in policy makers' assessment of collaboratives. First, policy makers view the boundaries between organizations as fluid, easily transcended. Second, policy makers assume that organizations are framed in terms of legislative and legal mandates, which, in turn, define the patterns of rules, roles, relationships, and measures of success by which individuals work. These assumptions underlie beliefs that policies can effect change and the pattern of rule and behavior. Consider these points relative to the assumptions framing collaborative theories of practitioners.

ASSUMPTIONS OF PRACTITIONERS ABOUT COLLABORATION

Although both the policy maker and the practitioner discuss collaboration in terms of concrete examples, the perspective of the practitioner differs significantly from that of the policy maker in several regards. This difference is not surprising because the circumstances of their work and responsibilities are very different. The term practitioner is used here to refer to those individuals who implement policy and are responsible for the production and delivery of services to clients. Thus, teachers and school administrators are defined as practitioners, as are social workers. District administrators represent something of a hybrid between policy makers and practitioners since they are responsible for both the implementation of state policies and the formation and administration of district policies. For the purpose of this discussion, we focus on those professionals responsible for front-line duties: the delivery of services that immediately involve clients.

The following are six assumptions that are widely identified by practitioners as essential to successful collaboration (see, for example, Melaville & Blank, 1993). The key idea underlying these propositions is the view of collaboration as social relations among practitioners. Successful collaboration requires involvement of the right people; people who are capable of leading others and showing them the potential of collaborative ventures. Such involvement ensures that people buy into collaborative projects and creates the political climate necessary to sustain commitment.

- Practitioners assume that collaboration is a process of identifying and articulating shared values and goals.
- Practitioners assume that successful collaboration is developing a sense of trust and ownership in the effort.
- Practitioners assume that successful collaboration is a process of conflict management and resolution.

■ Practitioners assume that successful collaboration is a learning process.
■ Practitioners assume that successful collaboration is largely a matter of human relations in addition to the overt purposes and goals.
■ Practitioners assume that successful collaboration requires that the "right" people be involved.

In other words, practitioners view collaboration as moving people toward collective action. This action is frequently described as a learning community (Sergiovanni & Starratt, 1993). Practitioners recognize the difficulty of sustaining change but unlike the policy makers, who see change as a legal and institutional matter, practitioners view change more as a matter of individual initiative and collective action.

Collaboration is viewed as achievable and productive; yet a thoughtful practitioner struggles to define a theory of collaboration. Often, the participants assume that a shared vision of collaboration exists without taking time to define what it means for themselves or for their purposes. Practitioners do not assume that the skills for collaboration exist within the organization, as many policy makers do. Restructuring, in this view, is achieved through the acquisition of skills, which in turn alter the patterns of rules, roles, relationships, goals, and expectations.

In this section, the differing assumptions that underlie the beliefs about collaboration for policy-makers and practitioners are highlighted. In the following section, the ideas introduced previously are expanded by framing explanations for why successful collaborations require shared values as well as new administrative structures and laws. Proposals for collaboration do not, generally, specify how or why shared values benefit collaborative action. The theory introduced is a step in this direction.

The literature describing collaborative organization has a long history. In the early 1960s, the literature was dominated by organizational theories that sought to explain the effectiveness of collaboration by examining their structure: size, wealth, and so forth (Hughes, Leonard, & Spence, 1972). Next, the literature used resource-dependency theory to explain collaborative ventures (Aldrich, 1976). Later theories reflected ideas of strategic management (Hill & Wolfe, 1994) and symbolic versus functional support (Deal, 1985; Meyer & Rowan, 1977). Changes in the capital structure of business (the global economy) have lead some to suggest that the old paradigm of organizations, which was a simple hierarchy of authority, has been replaced with networks of smaller organizations seeking short-term exchange agreements through "just in time management" (Forgsgren, Hagg, Hakansson, Johanson, & Mattson, 1995; Jones, Hesterly, & Borgatti, 1997).

These theories tend to ignore, however, the issues and concerns of managers and employees within the organization attempting to produce and deliver a service or product to their clients. During the 1970s and 1980s, a number of economists began focusing attention on the economics of organization and provided insight into why organizations adopt the structures they do (Hoenack, 1983). These theories are often framed against the backdrop of the market, which is to ask why economic exchanges are regulated within structured hierarchies (firms and organizations) instead of within the free market. The question is particularly appropriate to the study of collaboratives among social service agencies because the proposition requires individual agencies to abandon aspects of their hierarchical structure and adopt a more market-based approach to production and delivery. Economic theories of organization highlight important issues that help to explain why shared values are critical to the success of collaborative organizations as well as new governance structures, like the intermediate hierarchies we found in our case studies. In the next section, these ideas are introduced and set the conceptual framework by which we examine the case studies that follow. Additionally, this framework is used in the analysis and discussion of the case studies.

TRUST, COLLABORATIVES, AND TRANSACTION COST THEORY

Trust is an extraordinarily important element to the successful organization. Organization, in this chapter, refers to the linkages between individuals. Organization is not simply the hierarchical structure of authority or the boundaries of production that might be associated with some industry or social service. Public schools serve as a good example for clarification. The organization is not simply the hierarchy of authority among district administrators, school administrators, and teachers. Rather, organization is the social fabric, the nexus of agreements, that binds people together as they share resources for the many purposes and objectives served by those linkages.

Trust is at the heart of collaborative organizations. Where trust is high, individuals can spend their time and creative energy completing the jobs for which they are responsible. In an environment with high levels of trust, relatively little time is devoted to making sure that people are doing what they have agreed upon; that they are not reneging on an agreement. Trust ameliorates the need for contractual agreements and reduces the cost of negotiation and monitoring. Trust is a lubricant for social organization; without it, the frictions associated with contracting, negotiating, and monitoring would be so high that organization would be more trouble than it was worth.

It is not our purpose to define the concept of trust but to link it to the idea of shared values. We believe that the idea of shared values identified by practitioners as critical to successful collaboration is related to the idea of trust as introduced. The point is that these ideas have an economic relevance for how organizations are structured and organized; that the promotion of trust reduces transaction costs (a concept defined later in the paper) and allows for less formal and legal forms of governance (organizational structure). To help make these points, the following section discusses four key ideas related to collaboration, which we use to frame our thinking about collaboration.

Cornerstones of Collaboration: Collective Action, Rationality, Self-Interest, and Opportunism

Four ideas establish cornerstones for the model of collaboration we describe. The first is collective action. Collective action is almost synonymous with the way we think about collaboration, which suggests that if every one acted for the benefit of the collective then collectively all would benefit. Thus, the logic of collective action assumes that if an action is in the collective interest of a group, and if the members of the group are rational, then the group must be collectively rational (Hardin, 1982, p. 2). The apparent rationality of this argument obscures an important point of confusion. The confusion lies in an assumption that one can think about the behavior of groups in the same way that one thinks about the behavior of individuals, and, further, that groups have a collective will or interest. Collective action is viewed in this perspective simply as the aggregation of individual decisions to collaborate.

Decisions or choices, which are rational relative to the interests and goals of the individual, may not necessarily be rational for the group. This point is commonly made with reference to the "prisoner's dilemma" problem, where the interests of the individual are pitted against the collective. This dilemma is familiar to us all because individual rationality suggests a course of action that conflicts with the interests of the group. Such is the point made by novelist Joseph Heller in his book *Catch-22*.

The incentive for individuals to pursue their self-interest within a collective is obvious. If every individual in a group contributes to a collective purpose then every individual would derive some benefit. If all but one individual in the group contributes to some collective action, however, then the group suffers very slightly, while the individual who refuses to contribute gains the benefits of collective action without the cost of his or her efforts. Examples of such rationalized reluctance toward voluntary action are all around us. Collectively we all want clean air but individually we are reluctant to pay for the costs of controlling automobile emissions. We are all concerned about the problem of over-fishing the oceans but individually we like cheap prices for fish. This incentive for the individual to shirk his or her duties creates problems for the organization. Indeed, it is the basis for organizational hierarchy.

Where the opportunity for shirking, or even cheating, arises, the collective must do something to protect itself. In a mundane but illustrative example consider why restaurants automatically add 15 percent service charge to bills of parties of six of more. This stipulation constrains discretion and choice. The problem is that when it is difficult to assess whether or not an individual has voluntarily contributed to the collective welfare (in this case, everyone's obligation to contribute to a tip), the opportunity for shirking is easily rationalized. The specification of specific responsibilities is a relatively easy solution to an otherwise complex problem to manage.

Transaction Cost Theory and Collaboration

Hardin (1982) makes the interesting, and somewhat ironic, point that the general logic of collective and voluntary action is essentially grounded in the logic of market exchange and efficiency. Where a large number of buyers and sellers, a la Adam Smith's view of markets, exist, the market protects consumers from collusive agreements. A free competitive market ensures that goods and services will be produced at a fair and equitable price, since anyone trying to charge more than the market will bear will be pushed out of business by the collective action of not purchasing the higher priced good or service. Indeed, the fundamental idea is that a free competitive market ensures collective action that promotes efficiency, equity, and liberty.

The promise of markets and voluntary collective action seems so great that one might be inclined to ask why everything is not structured in collaborative networks of collective interest. Such was the question posed by Coase (1937) in the early 1930s: why do individual organizations exist? Why are activities that should be horizontally structured within the market of voluntary exchanges organized into vertical hierarchies under centralized control? These are the very questions we ask of social service agencies that seek to establish networks of organization through interagency collaboratives. In other words, why is it that organizations that can best serve the interests of their clientele through horizontal linkages are structured in vertical hierarchies? According to Coase (1937), vertical hierarchies, independent firms with clearly defined hierarchies of authority, exist because of the ubiquitous costs associated with coordinating activities through a less than perfect market place. These costs are described as transaction costs and efforts to minimize them affect social service agencies as well as for-profit firms.

Thus, one of the tenets underlying economic theories of organization is that organizational form is sensitive to cost factors and that, over time, individuals will seek organizational forms that are comparatively effective and efficient. The idea is not unfamiliar to anyone who has worked with a group of people on committee assignments or other tasks. The form or structure of organization will be adapted such that the most work, especially the administrative red tape that no one likes to do, gets done with the minimum effort. Where over time people learn new ways of organizing, they will introduce those ideas and attempt to implement them. A driving force of governing structures in both single and collaborative organizations is efficiency.

This basic idea is present in a number of economic theories of organization (see Barney & Ouchi, 1986, for a good introduction to these theories). In this study, we specifically focus on the ideas associated with transaction cost theory, which was pioneered during the 1970s and 1980s by Williamson (1975, 1984, 1986, 1995). The ideas in this theory are particularly appropriate to the concerns we bring to the study of collaboratives because the underlying premise of these ideas is that a fundamental relationship exists between the choice of governance structure and the cost of its operation. Governance structures refer to the organization of activities and rules by which individuals seek to produce and deliver goods and services. The choice between a collaborative governance structure or some type of hierarchy is not predicated on a willingness to collaborate as much as on the cost of alternative structures compared to the cost of governing in a hierarchy.

More recently, Milgrom and Roberts (1990) contributed to this body of theory by arguing that the cost of bargaining, a form of transaction costs, can be controlled more efficiently within organizational structures as compared to the costs associated with such transactions within a market environment (see, additionally, Pearce, 1997). The concept of bargaining is defined as those activities associated with the formation of agreements. The transaction costs in this perspective are identified as those costs associated with coordinating, contracting, and monitoring activities within and between organizations.

Problems of bounded rationality and information asymmetries underlie the cost associated with negotiating, monitoring, and coordinating. Simon (1955) describes bounded rationality as cognitive limitations that prevent people from working with perfect information even if it was available. In other words, even if perfect information existed, people could not make good use of it. Moreover, as Williamson and Masten (1995) observes, what information is available is often distributed unevenly among exchange partners. These information asymmetries create opportunities for unfair exchanges among collaborative partners. Ring (1996) notes that the problems of bounded rationality and information asymmetries are especially problematic for collaborative ventures, where success often requires large amounts of shared information to promote the collective interest and protect each organization's self-interest. Thus, a prudent member of a collaborating party may be wise to seek an agreement or contract as a way to protect himself or herself. The negotiation and writing of a contract can be costly and its effectiveness depends on whether or not it is monitored and enforced. Together, these problems represent significant costs associated with collaborative action. Coase (1937) and Williamson and Masten (1995) maintain that where individuals engage in repeated exchanges over time, it is not surprising that efforts to economize (find efficiencies) are pursued through the formation of vertical hierarchies.

Within this context, consider the problems of structuring an organization that draws resources from a variety of state-sponsored social services to address problems that are important for a common clientele but for which none of the agencies is wholly responsible. Imagine the risks associated with contributing resources, employee time, reputation, and other contributions, to a productive enterprise over which no single organization has control. The marvel is that any interagency collaboratives are formed, let alone that some succeed in coordinating activities with impressive results.

In summary, there is no more efficient organizational design than that structured around trust. Even if such a design is possible, trust is not sufficient to govern all organizational activity. If these collaborative organizations spend all their time monitoring collaborative activities to protect their interests, there is little time left for promoting collective interests. Thus, the question we ask is how do interagency collaboratives manage the problems of ownership, self-interest, and the costs of collaboration. How do they seek structures by which to govern the problems associated with sharing risk and accounting for the work of individuals who are not owners of the resources they use? How are the interests and goals of the group protected against the interests and goals of the individuals asked to do the job representing the group?

These questions are central to the success and survival of collaborative organizations lest the cost of working together overwhelm potential benefits, particularly when those benefits do not necessarily address the responsibilities of an individual agency's charter. In the next section, we describe our observations of the organization and work of eight large collaboratives from around the country. This description is then analyzed using the lens of transaction costs economics. The purpose is to reveal the presence of these costs and functions as they influence collaborative organizations. The chapter concludes with policy recommendations.

CASE STUDIES

The eight cases (Table 3.1) represent interagency collaboratives from five regions of the country: northeast, midwest, deep south, mountain west, and southwest. Populations of the communities studied varied from 100,000 for a collaborative in a single city to over 9,300,000 for a state level collaborative. The collaboratives were located mostly in urban centers, but one collaborative combined stakeholders from both urban agencies and agencies in adjacent rural areas. The collaboratives were evenly divided in their focus on educational issues exclusively or on broader community based issues, such as health and social services. Each of the collaboratives had been offered supplementary funds from the Pew Charitable Trust (through the American Association of Higher Education [AAHE]) for training of staff and for educating CEOs about the process. The initial sessions required the attendance of the CEO and at least one staff member from the initiating organization; participants were funded by the Trust. As the training continued, staff members were allowed to attend without their CEOs, who were either college/university presidents or superintendents of school districts. CEOs from other agencies, such as health care or law enforcement, were not involved at these stages of development.

The training AAHE training sessions were open to any communities who wished to explore the possibilities of collaboration across agencies for coordinating edu-

TABLE 3.1.
Overview of Cases

Case	1	2	3	4	5	6	7	8
Size	1 City	1 City	1 City	1 City	3 Counties	1 City	1 City	State
Region	West	N East	N East	Midwest	West	South	S West	Midwest
Population	100,000	140,000	161,000	179,000	222,000	265,000	600,000	9,300,000
Type	Rural	Urban	Urban	Rural	Combined	Urban	Urban	Combined
Focus	Community	Education	Education	Education	Education	Community	Community	Community

cational services to students from prekindergarten to college levels (PK–16). The initial focus on the training was to create a "seamless" educational system from PK–16. The concept of a "seamless" education centered on coordination of students' movement from one level of education to another and on services that could facilitate such movement. Primary emphasis was placed on successful matriculation of students from high school to college. When community representatives began superimposing a broader vision of the purposes of community collaboration, the focus of the discussion shifted from education to coordination of health, social service, and related agencies. Consequently, the relative emphasis on strictly education issues versus broader community-based issues varied among collaboratives. Because of this difference in scope as well as the difference in size of the initiatives, the research began as a study of the differences in organizational structures among the collaboratives. Initially, the researchers anticipated differences in the structure and process of collaboration among collaboratives. In studying each of the cases, however, these anticipated structural differences were not found. Instead, the structures for governing the collaboratives were markedly similar; it is the striking similarity among governing structures that prompted this discussion. If each of these successful collaboratives has moved to similar structural responses to interagency collaboration, then we can learn from their collective experiences.

The structures of these eight collaboratives were analyzed to offer the following description the evolution of community compacts. The establishment of these community-based collaboratives followed a relatively distinct pattern with only minor variations. The collective "story" offers an overview that can inform both stakeholders and policy makers about interagency collaboration.

Methods and Data

Through specific paths of qualitative analysis, called ethnographic content analysis (Altheide, 1987) and event structural analysis (Bakeman & Gottman, 1986), the conceptual process of collaboration was analyzed in the context of interagency collaboration. Ethnographic content analysis and event structural analysis allow one to move back and forth between data analysis and concept development by studying events, relationships among events, and the structure of the events.

Data were collected from archival sources and related documents including copies of collaborative agreements, organizational charts, charters, agenda of meetings, minutes of meetings, newsletters, and letters or memos among the stakeholders. Additional data were gathered through nonparticipant observation while attending meetings of the collaboratives' directors and CEOs. Finally, data were gathered through observation and note taking in a participant observer role in attendance at training sessions for initiating collaboratives in communities. Training materials used in these sessions provided additional data for the cases.

Data from the eight interagency collaboratives were individually analyzed and then cases describing the development and implementation of the collaboratives were developed. Overriding themes from the cases regarding the processes, structures, and organizational conditions that emerged in these collaboratives were then identified. The cases were compared to each other to identify similarities and dissimilarities, and the findings were synthesized to provide a conceptual framework for understanding the structural responses of interagency collaboratives to the requirements of the tasks identified.

Forming a Community Compact: Prepolicy Phases

In each community, the impetus for moving toward a collaborative effort to improve the education of young people stemmed from a widely held perception that the community had serious problems that were not being adequately addressed by any single agency or constituency. In each case, the initiators of collaboration were educators from prekindergarten to college levels. The discussion began with a focus on improving education and, in some cases, remained focused only on education. The focus of three collaboratives was expanded however, to include community concerns such as curfews, health care, and childcare. The variance of issues and focus among collaboratives makes sense when viewed through constructivist lenses that characterize these collaborations as collective meaning making. It is important to note here that although the focus varied somewhat, it was bounded in all cases by the initial reason for coming together—the welfare and success of young people in the community. In that sense, the focus of all collaboratives was comparable.

Various issues emerged from a series of meetings, each with a growing number of stakeholders who voiced concerns. Convening these meetings set the stage for continued dialogue and began to establish trust for continued participation among representatives from the various organizations. As mentioned, these meetings were held by a small group of educators who functioned as an organizing core team. Every core team included representatives from public and higher education, initially, and expanded to include representatives from business, government agencies, or the community as the effort took on momentum. That educators initiated and continued to play a major role in the development of collaboratives reflects, first, the congruence of their organizational goals with the goals of the collaborative and, second, the extent to which educators are held primarily accountable for the welfare of young people. Both of these factors in turn make educators more vulnerable to public outcries for reform and create motivation for their participation in interagency collaboration. Through interagency collaboration, educators could share the load and, if need be, share the blame for shortcomings usually attributed to education alone.

After three to five shorter meetings, a retreat-style gathering was organized to begin formal articulation of shared vision and purposes. In six of the eight cases, this meeting was conducted by a paid facilitator, trained in methods for allowing everyone to have a voice and then synthesizing the voices into common themes and an agenda for action. While keeping the overall vision in mind, the collaboratives had to identify a starting point. Starting points were identified in two ways: by selecting populations of students such as those in secondary schools, or by targeting particular high need areas of the community.

During this retreat-style meeting, stakeholders asked more questions than they answered. These questions and others guided the critical collection of data to clarify emerging issues. Sample questions follow. What is the drop out rate for our community? Is it even across schools? How does our drop out rate compare to national averages or to state averages? What problems most seriously hinder students' success in schools in our community? At which age should we focus our attention to make the most impact? Questions that were not directed specifically toward information gathering were directed toward identifying necessary tasks and negotiating who would be responsible for conducting those tasks. Participants were simultaneously assessing the risks and the costs involved and weighing those risks against the potential benefits. They were asking such questions as how much work will my organization (or myself) be required to do? What resources must we commit? What resources will be available to us? What are the direct short-term benefits and what are the long-term benefits of our participation? All of these questions illustrate the ongoing negotiation that was integral to collaborative effort. These finer points had to be agreed upon before the collaborative could move to address its major task of improving the success and welfare of young people.

Another activity at the retreat-style meeting was to identify existing partnerships and cooperative ventures and to discuss openly how these efforts would relate to the establishment of a collaborative. Often, stakeholders who were also participants of preexisting organizational programs addressing the purposes articulated in the meeting were protective of their success and reluctant to engage in any activity that might jeopardize their effort or usurp their recognition and potential for funding. At this juncture, one critical step was to bring CEOs of various organizations together to secure a public and formal endorsement of the pursuit of forming a collaborative. These CEOs in education and other agencies included the supervisors of all stakeholders or represented for profit and religious organizations that were influential in the community. As the general body of stakeholders began to see the overt endorsements of collaboration by their CEO, they were able to release ownership of previous efforts and merge those purposes with the collaborative effort at hand. If their CEOs did not overtly endorse the collaborative effort, stakeholders held to their previous effort instead of merging with the collaborative effort. For example, a politically influential Latino constituency had been promoting English as a second language endorsement for teachers in a particular district and had established an agreement with one university to offer such programs at a convenient school in the district. The Latino constituency not only secured a commitment from the university but had also secured external funding to bring an expert in from out of state to teach courses in a condensed format. The Latino constituency was reluctant to broaden this arrangement to include teachers from the other districts in the collaborative because the program was to be offered on a modified schedule to accommodate teachers in that district. They feared that expanding the student population might jeopardize the program by increasing the class sizes and causing other changes to the schedule. When the superintendent of that district voiced a similar reluctance, the Latino constituency stuck with their original plan to endorse teachers only from that district. Later, when the superintendent learned that the university might discontinue the program due to the small number of students involved, he publicly endorsed broadening the program to include teachers from other districts. This expansion was swiftly accomplished with the approval of the Latino constituency. Although this example illustrates the power of public, or symbolic statement, it also illustrates the ongoing negotiation in collaborative efforts to avoid risk and coordinate resources, including information resources. In fact, negotiations to reduce uncertainty or risk and the continuing quest for information constituted much of the work of the collaboratives at this stage. In summary, the continued overt and symbolic endorsement of the collaborative effort by the CEOs became an essential element in reducing the human "costs" of collaborative work.

Some stakeholders opted out of the dialogue either temporarily or permanently as a result of their assessment of the costs relative to the benefits to themselves and their organizations. New stakeholders who were not included in the initial meetings often joined the dialogue. In each of the eight cases, the process remained open and fluid. The initiators of the process viewed prescriptive or exclusive lists of participants as likely to cause the process to fail. Issues of trust were discussed in the final meetings before the formal agreements were signed; trust was actually on the agenda as an item for discussion at one of the training sessions for directors (AAHE, 1996). The participants in each of the collaborative efforts explored here were adamant both about the need for fluidity of the process as well as the competing need to bring closure and clarity to the dialogue. Various group processing techniques were employed among the cases, but each emphasized the need for a trained facilitator to reduce the time required to bring closure and to assure the successful synthesis of the collective voices. In other words, the facilitator was viewed as a necessary initial cost that resulted in an overall reduction of costs and complications over time.

Through the dialogue and the process of gathering ideas from all participants, the central values and shared purposes of the collaborative were gradually articulated. The stakeholders set down these central values and purposes in writing for public review. A sample of the wording of an overarching purpose for interagency collaboration is "leaders from education and the broader community have pledged to work together over the next six years to put in place a set of systematic reforms designed to increase dramatically the number of minority and poor students who complete high school, enroll in post-secondary education, and complete at least two years of college" (AAHE, 1996). A statement similar to this one framed the formal agreement among the agencies in all cases studied. This broad type of statement was then supplemented with specific goals such as this social and health services objective, "Middle and high schools will form small vertical units, matching students with counselors for a three or four year period of counseling and advisory needs" (AAHE, 1996). The collaboratives' overarching purposes with the more specific objectives were drafted into a formal compact, which was publicly announced, endorsed, and signed by the CEOs of each participating organization. In all eight collaboratives, this event was widely publicized and celebrated.

The group of CEOs who came together publicly to sign an agreement to collaborate also ultimately decided what resources were to be committed by each constituency. One prevailing characteristic of these eight collaboratives was that all of the collaborating organizations committed resources in one form or another to the collective effort. Constituencies that had participated in the dialogue and purpose-setting activities but could not participate in commitment of resources opted out of signing the formal agreement but remained supportive of the effort.

Formalizing the Collaborative: Policy in the Making

At this point, the formal organizational structures of the collaboratives emerged. The structures among the eight cases were not precisely the same, but the similarities among them are striking. Each collaborative identified a two-tiered intermediary hierarchy for coordination of the collaborative: (1) a symbolic structure composed of CEOs among the various organizations and agencies involved; and (2) a functional structure, which formed the nucleus of workers and paths for communication (Figure 3.1). The symbolic group brought the collaboratives to the forefront in the public arena and were instrumental in sending the political message that action was being taken to help youth succeed and that resources were being coordinated among several agencies. Their regularly scheduled meeting, ranging from once per month to twice a year, were publicized in the newspapers, on radio, and, in three cases, on the local television news. The composition of the symbolic group varied in number of CEOs included; the group membership averaged 16.3 members and ranged from 12 to 21 members. The symbolic group was given a variety of names: leadership group, steering committee, and advisory committee, to name a few. Because this group was largely symbolic in its role in governing the collaborative, a smaller "steering" subgroup of 5 to 7 CEOs emerged, which met directly with the directors of the collaboratives to monitor and coordinate activities. Interviews revealed that the directors sought this connection with a subgroup as a method of securing approval for ongoing work, for gaining authority for certain decisions, or for solving administrative problems that did not require a decision from the whole symbolic group.

The functional tier of the hierarchy acted as the conduit for flow of information across organizational lines and implemented procedures to address the specific objectives of the collaboratives. The director was a member of this group and met with them regularly, from once per week to once per month, to coordinate and

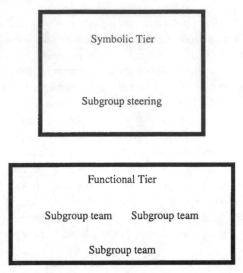

FIGURE 3.1.   Governance structures for collaboratives two-tiered hierarchy.

monitor their work on behalf of the CEOs. The functional group was also given a variety of names: working committee, strategic planning committee, design team, task force, as well as others. The functional group was also divided into subgroups that focused on specific tasks. For example, the subgroups for one collaborative were mathematics, science, and communications curriculum; parent/family commitment; professional development; incentives; and advising/mentoring. In every case, the collaborative created a functional structure for conducting the work of the collaborative, and those structures had similar staffing patterns.

Staffing

The formal designation of intermediate hierarchies was accompanied by the designation of staff members to support the collaborative. The number of staff members assigned to support each collaborative was 2 to 15 full-time equivalents (FTEs), ranging from the smallest to the largest collaboratives. All collaboratives appointed at least one director, and every collaborative had at least one clerical staff member to support coordination with who was hired by the collaborative. This staff member performed typical secretarial duties on behalf of the collaborative such as receiving and making calls, conducting written correspondence, arranging meetings, and handling invoices. Each collaborative also had one or more staff members reassigned to direct the functional tier of the hierarchy. Directors were selected from one of the core team members, and that person's time was reassigned as a resource to the collaborative.

A portion of the staff was composed of persons partially reassigned from their primary work organizations to the collaborative. The total number of persons partially reassigned from their respective organizations to the collaborative varied from 1 to 14 (0.5 to 3.5 FTEs) depending on the size and purpose of the collaborative. Reassigned staff came from three sources: university faculty, school district personnel, or state office personnel. This kind of reassignment was the source of much negotiation of duties among the functional hierarchy members. Each person reassigned attempted to define their role in relation to the collaborative and to simultaneously redefine their role in their primary work organization. This process of negotiating workload is discussed further in the analysis section.

In addition to persons hired for or reassigned to the collaborative, the work of many was affected or changed by the establishment of the collaborative. For example, a data-collection task force that included all of the research staff from the participating districts as well as the local college or university supported three collaboratives. In conclusion, the staffing of the collaboratives varied widely with the exception that all had one director and one staff, or a minimum of 2 FTEs, and all had access to additional staff for collection of data. Estimates of actual salary costs are difficult but it is reasonable to conclude that the costs staffing the collaboratives were substantial. The data do show that costs were greater than the core teams' original estimates.

Summary of the Collaborative Cases

Various like elements of the cases allow a collective analysis of collaboratives related to transaction cost theory. The work of the collaboratives is the same. Their structural response to organizing the work was an intermediate hierarchy with a

TABLE 3.2.
Working Assumptions About Interagency Collaboratives

Work and Purposes	Structure	Processes
Built consensus on shared goals for low SES students	Included broad coalition of community interests	Constructed meaning and language around shared goals
Gathered baseline student data	Established two-tiered intermediate hierarchy: functional	Shareholders negotiated workloads among themselves
Identified professional development needs	Educators formed core team	Created structures for efficient flow of information
Coordinated resources and services	Assigned full-time clerical staff	Overtly pursued trust building
Established individual and organizational rewards for participation	Reassigned professional staff for director and other roles	Established procedures for monitoring work and reporting progress
Sought additional resources	Resources contributed for shared use	

symbolic and a functional tier. Both the processes for establishing the collaborative and the processes for conducting the work of the collaborative were essentially the same. The profile, offered in Table 3.2, lists elements of successful collaboratives in terms of work, structure, and processes.

ANALYSIS: THE INTERSECTION OF CULTURAL AND ECONOMIC THEORIES OF ORGANIZATION

Elements of the cases, detailed above, provide an illustration of what is often described as "best practice." The experiences of these practitioners highlight the structures and processes that support successful collaboration. The promotion of "best practice" is generally associated with the hope that others will use the ideas in their efforts to create successful practice. Two problems confound such a hope. First, what is effective and just for one set of circumstances is not necessarily so in another organizational climate. Depending on the opportunities, constraints, personalities, costs, and resources of different collaborative organizations, the choices about how to organize will vary. The promotion of "best practice" mistakenly assume that organizational structure is a matter of individual volition. With evidence of what works, the individual is presumably responsible for creating similar structures of success.

Second, the promotion of "best practice" is largely framed in intuitive sensibilities and underdeveloped theory. Theory is intended to explain the complex and chaotic business of life. Theory provides a framework for focusing an individual's attention on issues that explain relationships. For example, theory should address the question of why the process of constructed meaning and language around shared goals is so central to the success of the collaboratives discussed in this chapter. The enumeration of best practices does not address such questions theoretically, except by suggesting that such practices work.

Sergiovanni (Sergiovanni & Starratt, 1993) attempted to explain best practice by arguing that the process of defining social and cultural values binds people together in a collaborative, rather than a self-interested, purpose. Sergiovanni labels these values as a kind of shared moral authority. Moral authority acts as a substitute for the bureaucratic authority of hierarchy. Professional autonomy, governed by moral authority rather than bureaucratic accountability, emerges in this view as the standard by which collaboration is structured. Sergiovanni's arguments hold an intuitive appeal that makes sense for many practitioners. But if we ask questions about why professional autonomy is important to collaboration and how moral authority improves practice, then the theoretical landscape begins to change.

Professional autonomy is about discretionary authority; who has the right to make decisions about how public (not private) resources are utilized, mixed, and sequenced. If that business of education and social work represent "nonroutine" tasks, as Brian Rowan suggests, then management cannot predict with certainty those tasks one needs to perform in order to maximize learning and socialization. Educators, who are close to the front lines of production (learning), have more and better information about what and how instruction should be produced and delivered. This appropriately places them in a good position to make decisions that enhance productivity. The idea of professional autonomy is as much about maximizing efficient production as it is democratic ideals.

The issues underlying Sergiovanni's concern about professional autonomy are fundamental to most social organizations: information asymmetries and the costs associated with gathering and utilizing information in an effort to coordinate productive activities. Collecting and utilizing information for any purpose carries with it a cost in time and effort. Where one party has an information advantage over a collaborative partner, there is always the chance for opportunistic behavior (taking advantage of the situation). The creation of a learning community, where stakeholders construct meaning and language around shared goals, improves the flow of information necessary for efficient production and reduces the chance of opportunistic behavior. Where these goals and values are institutionalized, in the way Sergiovanni describes as meta-values, then they command a moral authority around which professional autonomy can be implemented without the costly business of bureaucratic monitoring (or supervision as Sergiovanni labels it). These points help highlight the intersection of economic theories of organization with sociocultural theories.

The utility of shared values lies in their capacity to reduce transaction costs; those costs associated with the negotiation, contracting, and monitoring of complex exchanges. It is apparent in the case studies that the creation of community carries with it costs. Thus, as practitioners pursue the advantages of community, through the negotiation of common values and shared goals, they encounter the costs of such efforts. Economic theories of organization predict, reasonably we think, that individuals will seek ways of reducing such costs when possible. These are the analytic tools that help to explain why the pursuit of successful and efficient collaboration leads to the introduction of an intermediate hierarchy that governs the shared activities among constituent collaborative parties. The emergence of this organizational structure may be surprising to individuals who are not sensitive to the role of organizational structure as a device for managing costs. More critically, unless one sees the costs of collaboration, the role of structure as a cost-containment device is not relevant. It is only when economic and socioculture theories of organization are combined that the structures identified as "best practice" in these case studies begin to make sense.

Costs, Shared Goals, and Collaborative Structure

Central to the analysis of the case studies is the idea of cost. In this section, we highlight the presence and influence of costs related to the problems of negotiating, monitoring, and coordinating collaborative activities.

From the outset, stakeholders in each of the interagency structures entered into ongoing negotiations about the nature of the shared work and the degree to which individual organizational goals were congruent with interorganizational collective goals. Stakeholders negotiated over who would contribute resources and in what form, monetary or human. Individuals not only negotiated their role in the collaborative but also had to renegotiate work within their own organizations in order to devote adequate time to the collaborative. Their concern was how shifting work and time to the collaborative effort would impact those responsibilities for which their employer hired them.

The work of the collaborative was another example of ongoing negotiation. Just as stakeholders negotiated their individual interests, so they likewise negotiate on behalf of their host (employing) organizations. Some collaboratives focused exclusively on school-based support for educational endeavors; others focused on cleaning up drug activity and related violence outside of schools. The process of negotiating the work of the collaborative included much discussion about how individual organizational goals could be more efficiently met through the collaborative effort. If stakeholders decided that their organization's goals could not be efficiently met, they opted out. For example, the initial meetings of three collaboratives included representatives from small, private schools in the area. When in the discussions the focus of the collaborative on lower socioeconomic students and the expectation for contributing resources became clear, those representatives opted out of the dialogue.

Successful negotiation of the collaboratives' work was reflected in clearly articulated, shared values and goals that sufficiently embodied the collective and individual motivating incentives of the stakeholders. Further, only when the purposes of the collaborative were clearly articulated were the CEOs prepared to publicly endorse the efforts. In other words, only when the goals of the collective sufficiently encompassed the goals of individual organizations did the collective action proceed.

The CEO tier of the intermediary hierarchy provided a means for transcending the bounds of self-interest among individual stakeholders on the functional tier of the hierarchy. The formal announcement of the collaborative and public endorsement by the CEOs legitimized the work of the collaborative and, consequently, the work of individuals participating in the collaborative. When CEOs sanctioned the collaborative, employees were able to recognize that incentives related to promotion and being "in favor" with the CEO were directly related to their participation in the work of the collaborative. The willingness of the CEOs to recognize work for the collaborative with changes in job titles and release from regular duties was directly related to success of the collaborative.

Monitoring the progress of the collaborative effort was another source of cost for the collaborative. In a collaborative effort conceived as structure among equal partners, deciding who will monitor and report progress was issue laden. In each of the cases studied, the question of "who's in charge" was answered through the structure of staffing. The collaboratives created neutral or nonaffiliated staffing directly assigned to support the collaborative.

In addition to the nonaffiliated staff, every collaborative also had one director at the functional hierarchy level whose duties were officially reassigned to support the collaborative on a full- or part-time basis. The director was approved by the collaborative and was either hired from outside all constituent organizations or reassigned from an educational organization. In all cases, the director was an educator. The choice of an educator as director raised trust levels among stakeholders because of perceived goal congruence between the collaborative and educational organizations; stakeholders were less concerned with the possibilities of misuse of resources and had greater trust in the collaborative.

In cases where the responsibility for success of young people was viewed as shared among educational and other organizations, where educational success was substantially hindered by violence and drug related issues, noneducational organizations chose to fully participate in the collaborative and committed resources to the effort. In other words, the degree to which the individual organization's goals were congruent with the collective goals of the collaborative varied directly with the willingness of the organization to redirect internal resources to the collaborative effort in the name of efficiency, or reducing transaction costs.

Elements of Trust

Interagency collaboratives must include a number of safeguards for shared resources (Ring, 1996). The number of safeguards varies in relation to the degree to which the stakeholders are risk aversive. More risk aversive stakeholders require greater numbers of safeguards; less risk aversive stakeholders are more willing to view trust alone as a safeguard. One of the implications of such a view of trust as a safeguard may be that the successful collaboratives included more stakeholders who were willing to take risks and to view trust as an adequate safeguard for protection of an individual organization's resources. The notion that stakeholders are chosen at least in part because of personal characteristics and proclivity to risk taking became evident as one theme among the cases. Although interviews did not specifically reveal the criteria for selecting representatives, the data showed that care was taken in choosing the organizational representatives and that the choice was based on perceived aptitude for collaboration.

The element of time and its relationship to the development of trust cannot be overlooked in this discussion. Ring (1996) cites the repeatedness of transactions as allowing for development of trust that enables more valuable and meaningful levels of transactions over time. Ring further explores the notion of collaboratives as exchangers of information as a primary resource (1996, p. 14). These observations are relevant to the eight collaboratives studied in many ways. One critical theme became clear in the analysis of the eight cases: interagency collaboration takes times. Each of the collaboratives has evolved over 2 to 3 years of negotiating, and renegotiating, roles, relationships, and patterns of behavior. The articulation of shared goals as well as the initiation of the two-tiered intermediary hierarchies required several months and many meetings in which exchanges of information and negotiation of roles continued.

Structures were established for facilitating ongoing communication. As the traditional concept of organizing into isolated bureaucracies shifted to interconnected, more amorphous units, the constant source of structure appeared to be that found in ongoing flows of information. Inviting discourse on overriding educational issues helped coalesce like-minded people toward collective, coordinated action. Forums for collaboration became customary and comfortable. Trust among stakeholders increased. As important information became more commonly shared, that information became more perfect. Although the stakeholders were hampered by bounded rationality or cognitive limitations (Ring, 1996), shared knowledge reduced the costs of transactions and continued to promote trust among participants. Young (1992) refers to this shared knowledge as a shared linguistic community. Shared language offers an economy of words and preciseness of meaning that facilitates transactions across organizations, thus increasing trust and thereby, reducing transaction costs.

Creating an organization and maintaining a workable agreement requires effort. Recognition of this effort as a cost, and economic consideration, does not preclude recognition of sociocultural concerns commonly ascribed to collaboratives: shared goals. The creation and maintenance of shared goals is costly. This case study provides ample evidence that such costs exist. We document them as evidence supporting our claim that organizational structure is responsive to such costs. Recognition of this fact provides a strong explanatory model by which to understand why collaboratives operate as they do. It also provides insight into the relevance of trust in organizations.

CONCLUSION

The logic underlying the analysis of these cases is not intended to test transaction cost theory. Rather, the purpose of the analysis is to highlight the evidence that transaction costs shape the organizational behavior and structure of collaboratives. Our intention is to sensitize policy makers and practitioners to the presence of these factors influencing collaborative organizations. The way we think about complex social organizations is important because it shapes the questions we ask, the data we seek, and the inferences we draw from data (see Nisbett & Ross, 1980, for an excellent treatment of these issues). Too frequently, we seek simple causal relationships between complex policies and practices that are governed by multiple causal forces. Thus, explanations of culture and shared goals are obviously important elements to successful collaboration but they do not sufficiently address costs. Without recognition of the costs associated with these elements of collaboration, the ideas serve less as a theory (a guide for our thinking) and more as an ideology (thinking frozen in belief). The same can be said of economic theories of organization, which fail to recognize the sociocultural factors influencing organization and work. In this chapter, we recognize the existence of both sets of factors as they influence the organization and work of collaborative structures.

We argue throughout the chapter that organizational structure is important; it serves as a means by which to control costs. Structure reflects an agreement among members of an organization about how authority, protocol, and ownership are addressed. Collaboratives, and other resource networks, challenge the familiar bureaucratic structure of organizations, which assigns specific responsibilities in a division of labor and vertically integrates authority in a centralized hierarchy. Collaboratives are structured to realize the productive advantages of decentralizing authority. The interesting evidence in these case studies was that both horizontal and vertical structures were used as a way of governing the work generated by collaborative agreements.

The imposition of vertical governance structures (the symbolic CEO structures and the placement of directors over the work activities of the collaborative) provided a means by which to manage the costs associated with negotiating, contracting, and monitoring collaborative work (agreements). The creation of symbolic and functional structures to govern collaborative arrangements provided the means by which agreements could be maintained and operationalized without constantly renegotiating such matters. We describe these structures as intermediate hierarchies, which manage agreements between otherwise independent organizations. In this view, the intermediate hierarchy reduced the transaction costs associated with exchanges in the horizontal structures we call collaboratives. Coupled with the theory we discussed, the practice serves as a model for other collaboratives to consider. This is not to suggest that the structures developed by these collaboratives represent "best practice" and ought to mindlessly be copied. Rather, the practice provides a framework for mindfully attending to the issues that shape successful collaboratives, which include recognition of costs, sociocultural factors (language and values), and trust. We believe that failure to attend to the interaction of these issues helps explain why so many collaborative efforts fail to achieve their goals and end in dissatisfaction (Kusserow, 1991; Pearce, 1997). The role of intermediate hierarchy provides an important insight to how collaborative organizations address these issues successfully.

NOTES

1.   Numerous terms have been used to describe cooperative relationships between or among organizations. Among those terms are networked organizations or collaborative interorganizational relationships (Ring, 1996), joint ventures (Pearce, 1997), interprofessional collaboratives (Lawson, 1995), community compacts, and K–16 Councils (AAHE,

1992). In this paper, interagency agreements to collaborate and the resulting structures that support collaboration are called collaboratives for brevity. Stakeholders include anyone who has an interest in or who would be affected by collaborative action. Resources are the human, monetary, and in kind commodities exchanged in conducting the work of the collaborative.

2.   Obviously, this framework oversimplifies the reality of theory as well as practice. Most researchers rely on both inductive and deductive research strategies regardless of the framework used to define their work. Similarly, most practitioners will operate with some deductive/policy framework. Generally, however, this framework allows us to simplify reality, the hallmark of models of practice and theory, so that we can pursue our concerns.

REFERENCES

Aldrich, H. (1976). Resource dependence and interorganizational relations: Local employment service offices and social services sector organizations. *Adminstration & Society*, *7*(4), 419–454.

Altheide, D. (1987). Ethnographic content analysis. *Qualitative Sociology*, *10*(1), 65–67.

Association, N. G. S. (Ed.). (1990). *Educating America: State strategies for achieving the national educational goals: Report of the Task Force on Education*. Washington DC: National Governor's Association.

Bakeman, R., & Gottman, J. (1986). *Observing interaction: An introduction to sequential analysis*. Cambridge: Cambridge University Press.

Barney, J., & Ouchi, W. G. (Eds.). (1986). *Organizational economics*. San Francisco: Jossey-Bass.

Coase, R. H. (1937). The nature of the firm. *Economica, 4*, 386–405.

Crowson, R. L., & Morris, V. C. (1985). Administrative control in large-city school systems: An investigation in Chicago. *Educational Administration Quarterly, 21*(4), 51–70.

Deal, T. E. (1985). The symbolism of effective schools. *The Elementary School Journal*, *85*(5), 601–620.

First, P. F. (1996). Researching legal topics from a policy studies perspective. In D. Schimmel (Ed.), *Research that makes a difference: Complementary methods for examining legal issues in education* (pp. 85–109). Topeka, KS: National Organization on Legal Problems of Education.

Forgsgren, M., Hagg, I., Hakansson, H., Johanson, J., & Mattson, L.-G. (1995). *Firms in Networks: A New Perspective on Competitive Power*. Stockholm: Almqvist & Wiksell.

Hardin, R. (1982). *Collective action*. Baltimore, MD: The Johns Hopkins University Press.

Hill, S. C., & Wolfe, B. (1994, Winter). Managed competition: Issues and strategy. *The LaFollette Policy Report, 6*(1), 1–2.

Hoenack, S. A. (1983). *Economic Behavior Within Organizations*. Cambridge: Cambridge University Press.

Hughes, L. W., Leonard, J. R., & Spence, D. (1972). Educational cooperation: A perspective. *Journal of the National School Development Council, 1*(4), 4–9.

Jones, C., Hesterly, W. S., & Borgatti, S. P. (1997). A general theory of network governance: Exchange conditions and social mechanisms. *Academy of Management Review, 22*(4), 911–945.

Klein, S., Medrich, E., & Perez-Ferreiro, V. (1996). *Fitting the pieces: Education reform that works*. Washington, DC: United States Department of Education, Office of Educational Research and Improvement.

Kusserow, R. P. (1991). *Service integration: A twenty-year retrospective.* Washington, DC: Office of Inspector General, United States Department of Health and Human Services.

Lawson, H. A. (1995). Schools and educational communities in a new vision for child welfare. *Journal for a Just and Caring Education, 1*(1), ??

Mattessich, P. W., & Monsey, B. R. (1992). *Collaboration: What makes it work. A review of research literature on factors influencing successful collaboration.* Saint Paul, MN: Amherst H. Wilder Foundation.

Melaville, A. I., & Blank, M. J. (1993). *Together we can: A guide for crafting a profamily system of education and human services.* Washington DC: United States Department of Education, Office of Educational Research and Improvement.

Meyer, J. W., & Rowan, B. (1977). Institutionalized organizations: Formal structure as myth and ceremony. *American Journal of Sociology, 83,* 340–363.

Milgrom, P., & Roberts, J. R. (1990). Bargaining costs, influence costs and the organization of economic activity. In J. Alt & K. Shepsle (Eds.), *Perspectives on positive political economy* (pp. 57–89). New York: Cambridge.

Nisbett, R., & Ross, L. (1980). *Human inferences: Strategies and shortcomings of social judgment.* Englewood Cliffs, NJ: Prentice-Hall.

Pearce, R. J. (1997). Toward understanding joint venture performance and survival: A bargaining and influence approach to transaction costs theory. *Academy of Management Journal, 22*(1), 203–225.

Plant, R. W., & King, P. A. (1995). The family resource center: A community-based system of family support services. In B. A. Ryan, G. R. Adams, T. P. Gullotta, R. P. Weissberg, & R. L. Hampton (Eds.), *The family-school connection: Theory, research, and practice* (Vol. 2, pp. 288–314). Thousand Oaks, CA: Sage Publications.

Ring, P. S. (1996). Networked organization. A resource based perspective. *Studia Oeconomiae Negotiorum, 39,* 6–52.

Ryan, B. A., Adams, G. R., Gullotta, T. P., Weissberg, R. P., & Hampton, R. L. (Eds.). (1995). *The family-school connection: Theory, research, and practice.* (Vol. 2). Thousand Oaks, CA: Sage Publications.

Sergiovanni, T. J., & Starratt, R. J. (1993). *Supervision: A redefinition.* New York: McGraw-Hill, Inc.

Simon, H. A. (1955). A behavioral model of rational choice. *Quarterly Journal of Economics, 42,* 99–118.

Williamson, O. E. (1975). *Markets and hierarchies: Analysis and antitrust implications.* New York: Free Press.

Williamson, O. E. (1984). The economics of governance: Framework and implications. *Journal of Institutional and Theoretical Economics, 140*(SP), 195–223.

Williamson, O. E. (1986). *Economic organization: Firms, markets and policy control.* New York: New York University Press.

Williamson, O. E., & Masten, S. E. (1995). *Transaction cost economics: Policy and applications.* (Vol. II). London: Edward Elgar.

Young, R. (1992). *Critical theory and classroom talk.* Clevedon, England: Multilingual Matters.

part II
Students: The Bottom Line

4

FROM POLICY TO PERFORMANCE: WEAVING POLICY AND LEADERSHIP STRATEGIES TO IMPROVE STUDENT ACHIEVEMENT

Carolyn Kelley
University of Wisconsin-Madison

Tapestry is an ancient form of artistry in which colorful thread is woven into heavy cloth with rich detailed designs (Ackerman, 1970). To create a tapestry requires skill, materials, desire, a vision of the finished product, and a plan for achieving it. In many ways, creating policies that produce student achievement can be likened to weaving a tapestry, requiring appropriate skill, materials, determination, vision, and planning.

Whether or not policy makers weave a tapestry that produces high levels of student achievement (a masterpiece) depends on their ability to establish policy

The research reported in this paper was supported by a grant from the Pew Charitable Trusts No. 93-005234-000 and the U.S. Department of Education, Office of Educational Research and Improvement, National Institute on Educational Governance, Finance, Policy-Making and Management, to the Consortium for Policy Research in Education (CPRE) and the Wisconsin Center for Education Research, School of Education, University of Wisconsin-Madison (Grant No. OERI-R308A60003). The opinions expressed are those of the authors and do not necessarily reflect the view of the Pew Charitable Trusts, the National Institute on Educational Governance, Finance, Policy-Making and Management, Office of Educational Research and Improvement, U.S. Department of Education, the institutional partners of CPRE, or the Wisconsin Center for Educational Research.

and management systems that support student learning. This chapter explores the ways in which policy produces performance, and some of the factors essential to the development of educational policy tapestry as art.

POLICIES AS GOALS AND MEANS

Policies are defined as goals established by an organization or government that are applicable to a set of diverse actors within that organization or government, and the identification of means for attaining these goals (adapted from Pressman & Wildavsky, 1979). This chapter focuses primarily on state-level policies, although policies can also be established at other levels of government and within an organization. Policies may or may not be coordinated with one another, and they may or may not support a single vision of educational achievement. The challenge for educational policy makers is to weave together discrete policies that interlock with one another to produce a clear vision of student performance. Using the tapestry metaphor:

> The final, most complicated but most complete solution is the interlocked weave, in which the two different colored wefts are looped through each other at the point of contact. This leaves no slit, the fabric is equally solid and strong throughout, and the juncture is invisible, lending itself to the most finished realistic drawing (Ackerman, 1970, p. 304).

The imagery of tapestry suggests a tightly coupled and coordinated system, which is not consistent with images of educational organizations and policy environments as loosely coupled and ambiguous (Baier, March, & Saetren, 1988; Weick, 1976). The political environment of policy making and the need to develop coalitions of support around individual policies lend themselves to the creation of ambiguous, disjointed, and disconnected policies with distinct and sometimes conflicting goals (Baier, March, & Saetren, 1988).

By clarifying the nature and effects of various policy approaches, however, policy researchers have attempted to enhance policy makers' skill in weaving policy tapestries. In 1987, McDonnell and Elmore identified four policy levers, or instruments, that can be utilized by policymakers to transform goals into action.

> *Mandates* are rules governing the action of individuals and agencies, and are intended to produce compliance;
>
> *inducements* transfer money to individuals or agencies in return for certain actions;
>
> *capacity-building* is the transfer of money for the purpose of investment in material, intellectual, or human resources; and

system-changing transfers official authority among individuals and agencies in order to alter the system by which public goods and services are delivered. (McDonnell & Elmore, 1987, p. 158).

Policy makers communicate values and set agendas through these instruments, along with the use of their public positions, as bully pulpits for communicating the vision and values underlying policy choices (Wirt & Kirst, 1989). They can also create conditions conducive to achievement of policy goals by focusing these instruments to enhance coherence, capacity, and incentives for high levels of student performance (CPRE, 1998).

Coherence refers to the extent to which policies are woven together to support a common vision. Policy coherence implies alignment of policies with one another, so that they reinforce one another, rather than competing or lacking any particular focus. In this sense, *coherence* is preferable to *incoherence*. Policies should also focus the system toward positive behaviors rather than pathologic ones. For example, policy coherence around rigorous content, higher order thinking skills, and highly trained teachers is preferable to policy coherence around low level basic skills and unlicensed or ill-prepared teachers.[1]

Coherence should occur horizontally, so that various policies and practices reinforce one another *within* levels (e.g., the goals underlying state policies should reinforce one another and not be in conflict). It should also occur vertically, *across* levels of policy and practice, so that (for example) state curriculum guidelines, standards and assessments, district management practices, and school leadership and goals are conceptually linked.

Capacity is the presence or absence of appropriate human capital (knowledge and skills), physical capital (facilities and equipment), materials (curriculum), and financial resources (availability of funds, funding priorities, and centralization or decentralization of resource allocation decisions) needed to support educational achievement (Massell, 1998). Capacity influences the quality of policy decisions and their effectiveness. In addition, the level and type of capacity itself is determined by policy decisions over time.

Incentives refer to factors that motivate specific behaviors. Incentives may be intentional (e.g., relicensure requirements encourage continuing education) or unintentional (e.g., constantly shifting policy goals discourage teachers from embracing new reform initiatives), tangible (e.g., money) or intangible (e.g., pride in accomplishment). They can act to improve student achievement in two ways. First, incentives can directly motivate changes in behaviors, by both increasing and directing effort toward goal achievement. Second, incentives can create demand pressure from within the system to eradicate undesirable policies and practices. For example, when teachers have a stake in goal achievement, they are more likely to voice concerns about policies and management practices that impede their efforts to improve student learning.

FROM POLICY TO PERFORMANCE:
A CONCEPTUAL MODEL

A clear understanding of the ways in which policy affects performance can enhance the potential for policy makers to have a positive impact on student performance. The weavers (policy makers) need to understand how policies can be woven together to produce the detailed imagery of student achievement. Figure 4.1 illustrates a model of the ways in which policy and management produce student achievement. Actors in the *policy environment* include state and federal governments and professional associations. State policies tend to dominate the educational policy environment because states have the primary constitutional role in governing education, and states finance a disproportionate share of educational resources. Federal policies and professional associations also play an important role in the policy environment. For example, the certification of expert teachers by the National Board for Professional Teaching Standards reflects a significant trend in the preparation and career development of teachers. Similarly, the efforts by professional subject matter associations (e.g., the National Council of Teachers of Mathematics, or NCTM) to delineate best practices in curriculum and instruction have had a major impact both directly on the practice of teachers, and on the establishment of curriculum standards (Massell, 1994). Student achievement goals, and the means for achieving them, are communicated to districts, schools, teachers, students, and the public through these policies.

Policy makers have focused policy in a variety of ways to enhance student learning. These foci include teachers and schools, students, and strategic choices regarding governance and educational approaches. The evidence on the individual impact of these policies on student achievement suggest that they have small but significant impact on student learning. Promising teacher policies include standards and assessment policies (Archbald, 1989), incentives and accountability policies (Kelley, 1999), and teacher pre-service training and licensure policies (Darling-Hammond, 1998). Promising student-focused policies include high-stakes exami-

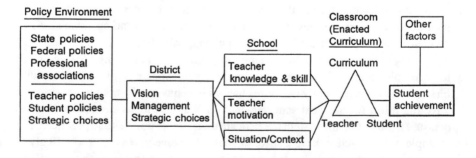

FIGURE 4.1.   From policy to performance.

nations (Bishop, 1998), graduation standards (Clune & White, 1992; Smithson & Porter, 1994), stronger school-to-work connections (Shapiro & Goertz, 1998), and higher education testing and admissions policies. Strategic choices include magnet schools, charter schools, and support for the adoption of education reform models, such as the New American Schools Designs (Odden, 1997).

District management plays an important role in shaping the student learning environment, and thereby influencing student achievement. Management plans, organizes, leads, and controls the behavior of individuals, groups and organizations to attain individual, group, and organizational effectiveness (Gibson, Ivancevich, & Donnelly, 1991). Effective district management strategies must negotiate the loosely coupled, bottom-heavy structure of educational organizations by establishing clear student achievement goals and decentralizing decision-making authority to the school level rather than utilizing hierarchical command and control strategies (Boyd, 1988). These decentralized management approaches are most effective when districts devolve knowledge, information, and rewards along with decision-making power to teachers at the school site level (Mohrman, 1994).

In a study of twelve instructionally effective school districts, Murphy and Hallinger (1988) found that these districts shared some common features, including conditions, climate, curriculum and instructional focus, and organizational dynamics. The factors are summarized in Table 4.1.

These characteristics are not inconsistent with the findings of Elmore (1997) in District 2 in New York, in which significant student achievement gains were attained through dynamic district leadership, a strong instructional focus, and a clear human resource management strategy (Elmore, 1997).

TABLE 4.1.
Characteristics of Instructionally Effective School Districts

Conditions	Climate
Labor peace	Productivity focus
Board support	Improvement focus
Community acceptance	Problem-solving focus
	Data driven
	Internally focused
Curriculum and instructional focus	Organizational dynamics
Goal-driven	Rationality without bureaucracy
Established instructional and curriculum focus	Structured district control with school autonomy
Consistency and coordination of instructional activities	Systems perspective with people orientation
Strong instructional leadership from the superintendent	Strong leadership with an active administrative team
Monitoring of instruction and curriculum focus	

Source: Murphy & Hallinger, 1988

As intermediaries between policy and schools, districts play a critical role in influencing the extent to which policies promote performance. Rarely purely supporting or purely impeding achievement of state policy goals (Firestone, 1989; Spillane, 1998; Wills & Peterson, 1992), districts can simultaneously act as a filter, a reinforcer, a competitor, and a blocker of policy implementation at the school level. To illustrate, a district might make important decisions in the allocation of state resources (filter), develop curriculum guides consistent with state standards (reinforcer), establish additional local educational goals inconsistent with state standards (competitor), and hold, rather than pass on to schools, information about grant opportunities (blocker). Districts also help to establish conditions, climate, focus, and dynamics; they control human resource policies; determine the overall goal direction of the district (and whether there is a clear goal direction); and determine the extent to which decisions are made centrally, or are decentralized to the school site level.

Together, policy and management practices establish goals and provide the means to shape the operation of schools. At the school level, three factors are particularly important influences of teacher and student performance: teacher knowledge and skills, teacher motivation, and the situation or context in which teachers work (Rowan, 1996).

There is mounting evidence that *teacher knowledge and skills* may be the single most important determinant of variations in student achievement (Darling-Hammond, 1998; Wright, Horn, & Sanders, 1997). Teacher knowledge and skills determine the ability of teachers to be effective in designing and delivering instruction. They are directly affected by teacher policies and management practices, most importantly pre-service training and licensure requirements (Darling-Hammond, 1998). In combination with these "gatekeeper" policies, human resource policies, such as recruitment, compensation, evaluation, and professional development also have an important impact on teacher quality.

Historically, teacher knowledge and skill policies have been weak and/or poorly enforced (Darling-Hammond, 1998; NCTAF, 1996). A number of efforts are currently underway to strengthen teacher knowledge and skills, including new approaches to professional development, teacher-directed models, and job-embedded professional development.[2]

Research has shown that for professional development to be effective, it must connect in an ongoing way to teaching practice. Professional development produced by educational reform networks in connection with the adoption of whole-school or sub-school education reform models is one approach that has been successful at providing ongoing professional development linked to educational reform efforts and to the specific school context. Other external providers include regional service centers established by states, professional networks of teachers, professional associations, and links to higher educational institutions (Massell, 1998; Slavin & Fashola, 1998).

A second approach is to attach consequences to the achievement of clear educational goals, and provide teachers with the time, opportunity, and control over professional development resources to enable *them* to make decisions about how best to focus their professional growth to meet student achievement targets (Massell, 1998; Odden & Busch, 1998). This strategy is likely to be particularly effective because of its potential to reinforce teacher commitment to addressing critical growth needs.

A third approach is a job-embedded professional development model, in which professional development is integrated with teaching practice. Performance-based licensure systems and the National Board for Professional Teaching Standards model this type of practice, in which professional norms dictate that teaching practice be research-based, outcome-focused, reflective, and thereby, involve professional growth throughout the teaching career.

Teacher motivation determines the level of effort that teachers exert, the focus of effort, and persistence toward the achievement of educational goals. As states and districts ratchet up expectations for student performance, teachers need to invest effort in redesigning curriculum and instructional approaches. Part of this reconfiguration requires that teachers have (or be able to obtain) the knowledge and skills needed to know how to modify their efforts. A second critical component is the motivation required for teachers to decide that it is worth their energy to invest in these modifications.

Figure 4.2 provides a model of motivation adapted from two established theories of motivation: expectancy theory (Vroom, 1964) and goal setting theory (Locke & Latham, 1990) (see Heneman, 1998; Kelley, 1998). The model shows the perceptual links between teacher effort and student achievement, and between student achievement and the consequences teachers associate with various possible student achievement outcomes.

The intensity, focus, and persistence of effort expended by the teacher is determined by teacher beliefs about the consequences of expending that effort. The more that a teacher perceives that working hard will pay off in higher student achievement, the more likely a teacher will be to exert that effort. Moreover, goals that are

FIGURE 4.2. A model of teacher motivation.

perceived as meaningful, clear, specific, and challenging will foster higher exertion of effort by teachers.

Intervening between teachers' beliefs about the effort–student achievement linkage are teacher knowledge and skills, and the situation or context in which teachers work. Conditions in the school that enable high levels of teacher motivation are discussed in the next section, but include things like principal leadership, professional development opportunities, and school culture.

Meeting or not meeting student achievement goals can be perceived by the teacher as leading to several consequences. To the extent that the teacher believes these consequences have a high probability of occurrence, the teacher will be motivated to receive positive consequences and to avoid negative consequences. Examples of positive consequences include public praise for achieving student achievement goals and a sense of pride and accomplishment from having students reach the achievement goals. Negative consequences might include heightened job stress, public displeasure with not meeting student achievement goals, and threats to job security.

The third school level factor is *the situation or context in which teachers work*. Context includes the structure, culture, and resources of the school. Some of the important structural features of effective schools include clear goals, school-site management, curriculum articulation and organization, meaningful professional development, and maximized learning time (Purkey & Smith, 1983). Schools also differ in organizational complexity (Firestone & Herriott, 1982; Herriott & Firestone, 1984), and student characteristics (Lightfoot, 1983), both of which can affect the ability of schools to embrace educational reforms. Some important cultural features include teacher collaboration or professional community, teacher learning, teacher efficacy, and teacher commitment (Louis, Marks, & Kruse, 1996; Rosenholtz, 1991). Principal leadership has been found to play a central role in developing these conditions in schools (Deal & Peterson, 1994; Elmore, 1997; Hallinger & Heck, 1996; Purkey & Smith, 1983).

Abelmann and Elmore (1998) find that school-level accountability systems play an important role in how teachers define their role in the organization. Internal accountability systems include both formal and informal aspects. An example of formal accountability is an evaluation system linked with performance expectations. Informal accountability includes the things that teachers hold themselves accountable for (individual responsibility) and the things that teachers hold one another accountable for (collective responsibility) within the school.

Together, teacher knowledge and skills, teacher motivation, and situation influence the extent to which the *enacted curriculum* will be effective at producing student achievement. Student achievement takes place through the enacted curriculum, which is the series of interactions between teachers, students, and the curriculum that occur over time. What students learn depends not only on the curriculum, but on the way that the teacher understands, interprets, and presents that material, and the attitudes and previous knowledge that the student brings to a series of teaching moments (Cohen & Ball, 1998). Thus, a student's knowledge of writing (for example) depends on a series of interactions between curriculum, teacher, and student over time. The artistry in producing excellent writers through policy is in cutting through the layers in the system enough to influence the ways in which teachers and students interact with curricular materials. Because teaching and learning are highly engaging tasks, these influences must be internalized by teachers so that they consciously influence curriculum and instructional decisions, and so that they influence the ways that teachers and students interact at a subconscious level as they engage in learning.

THE ART OF WEAVING A POLICY TAPESTRY

The artistry in weaving a policy tapestry is in combining policy, leadership, and management at the state, district, and school levels to create the knowledge and skills, motivation, and context that will result in meaningful interaction between teachers, students, and instructional materials in the teaching moment. This is why it is so difficult to make policy that has a clear effect on student achievement. Assuming that policies themselves are well designed (which can be a problematic assumption given the politics of policy formulation), policies must not only *penetrate* administrative layers, but district management must reinforce, accommodate, and not conflict with these policies; and teacher knowledge and skills, motivation, and school context must support policy implementation so that teachers purposefully and effectively incorporate these policies into their teaching practice, and internalize them enough to draw on them while engaging with students in the enacted curriculum.

Although there is no guarantee that any particular policy or management decision will impact the interactions between teachers, students, and the curriculum, and raise student achievement to higher levels, an understanding of the ways in which policy and management decisions produce achievement may help shape policy in ways that more readily produce high levels of student performance. Note that although the policy to performance framework implies causality *from* policy *to* performance, in practice, the student, the classroom, the school, the district, and the policy environment are co-equal and interdependent partners in the education and policy system. For example, as described previously, policy makers need to attend to issues of policy coherence, incentives, and capacity. They need to design policies that are sensitive to local context. The responsibility for coherence rests not just with policy makers, however, but with district level managers as well. District administrators need to *adapt to* the policy environment, but they also need to *work with* the policy environment to provide feedback and direction to policy makers to make good decisions about policy design. Similarly, policy and management decisions shape school-level factors, but teachers and principals also have a responsibility to students and the public to promote effective professional practice through their actions and by organizing to voice concerns about ineffective policies and management practices.

Together, as partners, these actors can work with policy makers to weave a policy tapestry of intricate and detailed design—a masterpiece of student achievement.

NOTES

1.   This conceptualization of coherence was adapted from remarks by Mary Kennedy, Michigan State University, in the CPRE Performance Review, September 10, 1998.

2.   Douglas Tuthill, Pinellas Classroom Teachers Association coined the term "job-embedded professional development."

REFERENCES

Abelmann, C., & Elmore, R. F., with J. Even, S. Kenyon, & J. Marshall. (1998). *When accountability knocks, will anyone answer?* Consortium for Policy Research in Education, Harvard University, Cambridge.

Ackerman, P. (1970). *Tapestry, the mirror of civilization.* New York: AMS Press.

Archbald, D. (1989). *State/district curriculum control systems and their effects: A preliminary analysis.* Paper presented at the Annual Meeting of the American Educational Research Association, San Francisco, CA.

Baier, V. E., March, J. G., & Saetren, H. (1988). Implementation and ambiguity. In J. G. March (Ed.), *Decisions and organizations* (pp. 150–164). New York: Basil Blackwell.

Bishop, J. (1998) *Do curriculum-based external exit exams enhance student achievement?* Philadelphia: University of Pennsylvania, Consortium for Policy Research in Education.

Boyd, W. L. (1988). Policy analysis, educational policy, and management: Through a glass darkly? In N. J. Boyan (Ed.), *Handbook of research on educational administration,* (pp. 501–522). New York: Longman Press.

Clune, W., & White, P. (1992). Education reform in the trenches: Increased academic course-taking in high schools with lower achieving students in states with higher graduation requirements. *Educational Evaluation and Policy Analysis, 14*(1), 2–20.

Cohen, D. K., & Ball, D. L. (1998). What is capacity for instruction and what is entailed in building capacity? Presented at the 1998 Annual Meeting of the American Educational Research Association, San Diego, CA.

Consortium for Policy Research in Education (CPRE). (1998). Improving the effectiveness of reform: the Consortium for Policy Research in Education. Paper prepared for the Office of Educational Research and Improvement, United States Department of Education. Philadelphia, PA: Author.

Darling-Hammond, L. (1998). Teacher quality and student achievement: A review of state policy evidence. Stanford University.

Deal, T. E., & Peterson, K. D. (1994). *The leadership paradox: Balancing logic and artistry in schools.* San Francisco: Jossey-Bass.

Elmore, R., with Burney, D. (1997). *Investing in teacher learning: Staff development and instructional improvement in community school district #2, New York City*. New York: National Commission on Teaching and America's Future and the Consortium for Policy Research in Education, Teachers College.

Firestone, W. A. (1989). Using reform: Conceptualizing district initiative. *Educational Evaluation and Policy Analysis, 11*(2), 151–164.

Firestone, W. A., & Herriott, R. E. (1982). Two images of schools as organizations: An explication and illustrative empirical test. *Educational Administration Quarterly, 18*, 39–50.

Gibson, J. L., Ivancevich, J. M., & Donnelly, J. H., Jr. (1991). *Organizations: behavior, structure, processes* (7th ed.). Homewood, IL: Richard D. Irwin, Inc.

Hallinger, P., & Heck, R. H. (1996). Reassessing the principal's role in school effectiveness: A review of empirical research, 1980–1995. *Educational Administration Quarterly, 32*(1), 5–44.

Heneman, H. H., III. (1998). Assessment of the motivational reactions of teachers to a school-based performance award program. *Journal of Personnel Evaluation in Education, 12*(1), 43–59.

Herriott, R., & Firestone, W. (1984). Two images of schools as organizations: A refinement and an elaboration. *Educational Administration Quarterly, 20*, 41–58.

Kelley, C. (1998). The Kentucky school-based performance award program: School-level effects. *Educational Policy, 12*(3), 305–324.

Kelley, C. (1999). The motivational impact of school-based performance awards. *Journal of Personnel Evaluation in Education, 12*(4), 309–326.

Lightfoot, S. L. (1983). *The good high school*. New York: Basic Books.

Locke, E. A., & Latham, G. P. (1990). *A theory of goal setting and task performance*. Englewood Cliffs, NJ.: Prentice-Hall.

Louis, K. S., Marks, H. M., & Kruse, S. (1996). Teachers' professional community in restructuring schools. *American Educational Research Journal, 33*(4), 757–798.

Massell, D. (1994). Setting standards in mathematics and social studies. *Education and Urban Society, 26*(2), 118–140.

Massell, D. (1998, July). State strategies for building local capacity: Addressing the needs of standards-based reform. *CPRE Policy Briefs*, RB25. Philadelphia: Consortium for Policy Research in Education, Graduate School of Education, University of Pennsylvania.

McDonnell, L. M., & Elmore, R. F. (1987). Getting the job done: Alternative policy instruments. *Educational Evaluation and Policy Analysis, 9*(2), 133–152.

Mohrman, S.A. (1994). High involvement management in the private sector. In Susan Albers Mohrman, P. Wohlstetter & Associates, *School-based management: Organizing for high performance.* (pp. 25–52). San Francisco: Jossey-Bass.

Murphy, J., & Hallinger, P. (1988). Characteristics of instructionally effective school districts. *Journal of Educational Research, 81*(3), 175–181.

National Commission on Teaching and America's Future (NCTAF). (1996). *What matters most: Teaching for America's future*. New York: Author.

Odden, A. (1997). Raising performance levels without increasing funding. *School Business Affairs, 63*(6), 2–10.

Odden, A., & Busch, C. (1998). *Financing schools for high performance: Strategies for improving the use of educational resources*. San Francisco: Jossey-Bass.

Pressman, J. L., & Wildavsky, A. (1979). *Implementation (2nd Ed.)*. Berkeley: University of California Press.

Purkey, S. C., & Smith, M. S. (1983). Effective schools: A review. *The Elementary School Journal, 83*(4), 427–452.

Rosenholtz, S. J. (1991). *Teachers' workplace: The social organization of schools*. New York: Teachers College Press.

Rowan, B. (1996). Standards and incentives for instructional reform. In S. H. Fuhrman, & J. O'Day (Eds.), *Rewards and reform: Creating educational incentives that work* (p. 195–225). San Francisco: Jossey-Bass.

Shapiro, D., & Goertz, M. E. (1998). *Connecting work and school: Findings from the 1997 National Employers Survey*. Paper presented at the Annual Meeting of the American Educational Research Association, San Diego, CA.

Slavin, R. E., & Fashola, O. S. (1998). *Show me the evidence! Proven and promising programs for America's schools*. Thousand Oaks, CA: Corwin Press.

Smithson, J., & Porter, A. (1994). *Measuring classroom practice: Lessons learned from efforts to describe the enacted curriculum—The reform up close study*. New Brunswick, NJ: Rutgers University.

Spillane, J. P. (1998). State policy and the non-monolithic nature of the local school district: Organizational and professional considerations. *American Educational Research Journal, 35*(1), 33–63.

Vroom, V. H. (1964). *Work and Motivation*. New York: Wiley.

Weick, K. E. (1976). Educational organizations as loosely coupled systems. *Administrative Science Quarterly, 21*, 1–19.

Wills, F. G., & Peterson, K. D. (1992). External pressures for reform and strategy formation at the district level: Superintendents' interpretations of state demands. *Educational Evaluation and Policy Analysis, 14*(3), 241–260.

Wirt, F. M,. & Kirst, M. W. (1989). *The politics of education: Schools in conflict*. Berkeley: McCutchan Publishing Corporation.

Wright, S. P., Horn, S. P., & Sanders, W. L. (1997). Teacher and classroom context effects on student achievement: Implications for teacher evaluation. *Journal of Personnel Evaluation in Education, 11*, 57–67.

5

EDUCATION AND CHANGING DEMOGRAPHICS

Betty Merchant
University of Illinois, Urbana-Champaign

As the new millennium approaches, American public schools appear to exemplify the adage, "The more things change, the more they remain the same." Despite the fact that the demographics of students enrolled in grades K–12 have changed considerably over the past several years, the demographic profiles of teachers and principals have remained remarkably constant.

According to data generated by the 1987–1988 and 1990–1991 Schools and Staffing Surveys (SASS) and the 1993–1994 School Questionnaire, in 1987–1988, 29.3 percent of public school students were classified as minority students; by 1993–1994, that figure had risen to 32.7 percent (U.S. Department of Education, 1996). Although the percentage of students enrolled in public schools who were classified as black, non-Hispanic was no different in 1993–1994 than it had been in 1987–1988 (16.3%), there was a marked increase in the percentage of students classified as Hispanic, from 9.4 percent in 1987–1988 to 11.9 percent in 1993–1994. The percentage of students classified as Asian rose slightly during this period, from 2.5 percent to 3.4 percent.

Data in the report indicate that the percentage of minority students in 1993–1994 varied considerably by community type, with 54 percent of the students in central city schools classified as minority, compared to 29.7 percent in urban/fringe schools and 18.9 percent in rural/small schools. Across all community types, a greater percentage of public schools than private schools reflected a racial-ethnic minority student population of 20 percent or more. Minority student enrollment in 1993–

1994 was also correlated with school size, in that larger schools tended to have a higher percentage of minority students than did smaller schools.

Table 5.1 provides an interesting look at the changes in the percentage of public school students identified as white between 1970 and 1996 in kindergarten, elementary, and high school (U. S. Bureau of the Census, 1998), with the percentage of white students decreasing across all grade levels by approximately 6 to 7 percent from 1970 to 1996.

When looking at the number of students ages 5 to 19 years enrolled in public and private schools combined, data from the U. S. Bureau of the Census (1998) indicate that from 1990 to 1996, the percentage of students classified as white increased by approximately 9 percent, black by almost 13 percent, and Hispanic by 36 percent.

There are additional changes occurring in the composition of the student population in our nation's public schools. According to *Conditions of Education, 1997*, in the 1993–1994 academic year, 46.3 percent of schools had students who were English language learners (National Center for Education Statistics, 1997a). The report also indicates that the number of children who were English language learners increased from 1.25 million in 1979 to 2.44 million in 1995. Approximately 60 percent of the schools in central cities and urban fringe/large towns had English language learners in that year.

Data from the U.S. Department of Education (1996) indicate that in 1993–1994 a higher percentage of English language learners in the public sector were found in central cities (9%) than in either urban/fringe (5%) or rural areas (2%). The data also revealed that public elementary schools in central cities reflected a larger percentage of English language learners (11%) than did secondary schools (6%). According to this report, whereas the percentage of schools providing bilingual programs decreased from 20.0 percent to 17.8 percent between 1987–1988 and 1993–1994, the percentage of public schools providing English as a second language (ESL) classes during this period increased from 34.4 percent to 42.7 percent. The most dramatic increase occurred in rural areas, where the percentage of schools that provided ESL programs increased by about 50 percent between school years 1987/88 and 1993/94 (National Center for Education Statistics,

TABLE 5.1.
Percentage of Students Classified as White in Public Schools in
1970, 1980, 1990, and 1996

	Year (percent)			
	1970	1980	1990	1996
Kindergarten	84.4	80.7	78.3	77.4
Elementary	83.1	80.9	78.9	77.4
High school	85.6	NA	79.2	77.9

1997a). These data leave no room for doubt about the increasing racial, ethnic, and linguistic diversity of the students enrolling in America's public schools.

Whereas the racial and ethnic composition of the public school student population has changed significantly over the last several years, the demographics of public school educators have remained remarkably stable. For example, according to the U.S. Department of Education (1996), in 1987–1988, 12.5 percent of teachers were classified as minority; in 1993–1994, the overall percentage had only increased to 13.5 percent. Despite the increased percentage of minority teachers in 1993–1994, 42.3 percent of the public schools in that year had no minority teachers on staff. Table 5.2 displays data obtained from *Schools and staffing in the United States: A statistical profile, 1993–1994.*

Additional data from the National Center for Education Statistics (United States Bureau of the Census, 1998) indicate that, in 1993–1994, white teachers accounted for 87 percent of the teaching force. Examining the percentage distribution of these teachers across years of teaching experience categories, 30 percent of white teachers had 20 or more years of experience, while 9.4 percent had 3 or fewer years of teaching experience. The percentage distribution of black teachers across years of teaching experience reveals that 35.2 percent of black teachers had 20 years or more of experience, whereas 8.5 percent had 3 or fewer years of experience. The percentage distribution of Hispanic teachers indicates that 17.1 percent had taught 20 or more years, while 16.7 percent had taught 3 or fewer years. More recent data from the National Education Association, indicate that, as of spring 1996, the percentage of public school teachers classified as white was 90.7 percent (National Center for Education Statistics, 1997b).

Data reported by the U.S. Department of Education indicate that the percentage of principals who are minority has changed very little in the past few years; from 12 percent in 1990–1991 to 14 percent in 1993–1994. Those classified as black, non-Hispanic made up 10 percent of the principals, whereas those classified as Hispanic accounted for only 4 percent of the elementary and secondary principals.

TABLE 5.2.
Percentage Distribution of Public School Teachers by Race-Ethnicity, in Schools With a Student Minority Enrollment of 20 Percent More, by School Type, 1993–1994

	Race-Ethnicity of Teacher (percent)				
	White non-Hispanic	Black non-Hispanic	Hispanic	Native American	Asian/Pacific Islander
Central city	68.4	18.2	10.8	0.5	2.1
Urban fringe/large town	80.3	9.7	6.5	0.9	2.6
Rural/small town	83.0	10.5	4.3	1.7	0.6

Source: U.S. Department of Education, 1996

TABLE 5.3.
Percentage Distribution of Public School Principals by Race-Ethnicity,
in Schools With a Student Minority Enrollment of 20 Percent or More, by School Type,
1993–1994

	Race-Ethnicity of Principal (percent)				
	White non-Hispanic	Black non-Hispanic	Hispanic	Native American	Asian/Pacific Islander
Central city	56.8	30.5	10.7	0.5	1.6
Urban fringe/large town	72.2	16.9	8.5	0.5	2.0
Rural/small town	81.3	11.3	4.9	2.2	0.3

Overall, schools with the most minority students tended to have the most minority teachers and principals. Table 5.3 contains a breakout of this data.

According to the U.S. Department of Education (1996) in 1993–1994, the percentage of teachers who are female has remained comparatively stable, from 71 percent in 1987–1988 to 73 percent in 1993–1994. Despite their numbers, however, the percentage of women principals has increased only slightly, from 35 percent in 1990–1991 to 39 percent in 1993–1994.

In addition to the increasing racial, ethnic, and linguistic diversity of the nation's young people, a growing percentage of public school students are presenting learning needs that require special education services. According to data provided by the United States Department of Education, Office of Special Education and Rehabilitative Services, and the National Center for Education Statistics, and reported in *The Condition of Education, 1996* (National Center for Education Statistics, 1996), the percentage distribution of children from birth to age 21 years who were served by federally supported programs for students who had specific learning disabilities more than doubled between 1977 and 1994. In contrast, the percentage distribution of children who had speech and language impairments and mental retardation decreased from 1977 to 1994, while the percentage distribution

TABLE 5.4.
Percentage Distribution of Children From Birth to Age 21 Who Were Served by
Federally Supported Programs for Students with Disabilities,
by Type of Disability; 1977, 1987, and 1994

	Year		
	1977	1987	1994
Specific learning disabilities	21.6	43.8	45.5
Speech or language impairments	35.3	26.0	18.8
Mental retardation	26.0	14.7	10.3
Serious emotional disturbance	7.7	8.8	7.7

of students who had serious emotional disturbance who were served by federally supported programs remained relatively stable during this period. Table 5.4 displays this data.

According to the National Center for Education Statistics (1996), the number of students participating in federal programs for children with disabilities has been increasing at a faster rate than total public school enrollment. While total public school enrollment decreased 2 percent between 1977 and 1994, the number of students participating in federal programs for children with disabilities increased 46 percent.

The data on the racial, ethnic, and linguistic composition of today's students reflect a clear trend in which young people historically categorized as "minority" now account for an increasingly large proportion of today's public school students. The evidence on hand suggests that this trend will continue well into the next millennium. In view of the current demographics of public school educators, this means that, increasingly, teachers and principals will be held responsible for addressing the academic and social needs of students who differ from themselves racially, ethnically, and linguistically. These differences may contribute to serious misunderstandings and conflicts between educators and students. Additionally, there is a danger that taken-for-granted educational policies and practices will be maintained without recognizing the importance of reexamining the ways in which these customary practices and policies (which may have worked well in the past) may now systematically disadvantage particular groups of students while advantaging others.

One conclusion that emerges from the data is that public school educators must develop a familiarity with and an understanding of the various racial and ethnic communities served by their schools. Based on the fact that the average age of public school teachers in 1993–1994 was 43.1 and that of principals was 47.7 (U.S. Department of Education, 1996), it is reasonable to conclude that a large number of men and women who are currently teaching and administering were not exposed to courses in multicultural education and student diversity during their pre-service training, which has now become a part of the professional preparation curriculum in most colleges and universities. Consequently, whatever these teachers and administrators know about issues of diversity has most likely resulted from either their own efforts or from in-service staff development activities provided by their schools or districts. Administrators are the designated instructional leaders in their schools; they must provide teachers with the resources and staff development opportunities they need to work effectively with diverse student populations.

Another conclusion that emerges from the data is that given the increasing numbers of English language learners enrolling in public schools, educators must, at a minimum, develop a baseline understanding of second language acquisition. Administrators who lack this understanding operate within a context of insufficient information about effective educational policies and practices for limited and non–English-speaking students, especially with respect to matching their instructional experiences with state and nationally mandated learning goals and objectives.

One of the more serious consequences of not understanding the process of second language acquisition is that teachers and principals often worry that students are talking about them in a negative fashion when they speak in their native languages; this often leads to feelings of defensiveness and a lack of trust in these students. Additionally, educators who do not know how to speak a second language frequently believe that English language learners understand more English than they are willing to produce; and that in effect, these students are trying to manipulate them by pretending to be unable to speak English. It is the case that comprehension precedes oral fluency, however, many educators unfamiliar with the language-learning process view this as a form of defiance. This, unfortunately, leads to negative feelings toward these students (Merchant, 1999). A lack of understanding about second language acquisition also results in teachers and administrators unintentionally perpetuating instructional practices and educational policies that are ineffective in helping English language learners achieve academically and socially.

In the past, classroom educators have not been held accountable for educating students with special needs; these students were assigned to specially credentialed teachers and relegated to the margins of the school community. With the national emphasis on public school accountability for the learning of all students, however, regular classroom teachers and administrators are now charged with sharing responsibility for the learning of special needs students. Administrators have a critical role to play in creating and nurturing a culture in which all teachers and staff members in the school feel personally and professionally responsible for ensuring the academic and social success of all of the children who are members of the school community. Administrators can stress the importance of shared responsibility through such actions as including the specially credentialed teachers in staff meetings, soliciting their involvement in school improvement plans, and scheduling time when they and the regular classroom teachers can meet with one another to explore methods of differentiating instruction for the special needs students in their room.

The data reported in this chapter on the percentage of elementary and secondary public school teachers in 1993–1994 who had been educators for 3 or fewer years reveal that a larger percentage of Hispanic teachers fit into this category than is true of white or black teachers. Among public school teachers with 20 years or more of full-time experience, a smaller percentage of Hispanics fell into this category than did those classified as white or black. In view of the fact that the Hispanic population is the most rapidly growing minority group in the United States, it is critical that administrators develop a strategy for recruiting and retaining Hispanic teachers, many of whom are new to the profession.

Administrators also play a critical role in developing a sense of community among teachers, students, and their families, and they need to develop the skills that will enable them to communicate effectively with parents of different racial, ethnic, and linguistic groups as well as parents of students with special needs. It is essential that all parents feel welcomed and supported by their children's teachers and principals and that they feel comfortable contacting the school with any concerns they may have about the academic and social progress of their children. Parents must also feel valued by the educators who work with their children and principals and teachers must take the time to get to know the parents in their communities, even if it means employing additional resources (such as a language translator) to communicate effectively with these parents.

An important aspect of the principal's job is that of reexamining the role of the school with respect to the communities it serves. For example, it may be necessary to provide adult classes in ESL at the school site in the evenings, for the parents of immigrant children who are not yet fluent in English. Such a program may also require providing child care services on site so that parents of small children can attend these ESL classes.

Unless administrators develop their own ability to work effectively with racially, ethnically, and linguistically diverse students as well as those with special learning needs, the academic and social potential of these students will be inadequately developed and that will result in huge economic and social costs—to the individual as well as to the society. A lack of administrative support of teachers who must respond to the needs of students whom they are ill-prepared to educate, will also result in the loss of teachers from the profession. Data from the U.S. Department of Education (1996) indicate that in schools with a minority enrollment of 20 percent or more, a higher percentage of teachers state that they definitely plan to leave the profession than is true of their counterparts in schools with a minority enrollment of less than 20 percent.

The changing demographics and increasing linguistic diversity of many school communities will place increased pressure on administrators, particularly monolingual English speakers, to assume a more dynamic role in instructional leadership activities. Administrators will have to become proactive in improving the capacity of their schools to work effectively with new groups of students. This will require principals to become increasingly sensitive to the importance of engaging all relevant participants in identifying the needs of students, parents, and teachers, and in examining which educational policies and practices continue to be effective and which need to be changed in order to improve learning conditions for all students. Administrators will have to assume an active role in monitoring the environment and obtaining a variety of perspectives on various issues, rather than depending on communication patterns and educational responses that may have been effective in the past but are no longer responsive to current conditions.

The changing demographics of today's public school students demand a genuine reassessment of school-wide curriculum, instruction, and evaluation and discipline policies and practices; this will require teachers and principals who are committed to providing a high quality learning environment for all members of the school community. The increasingly diverse student populations enrolling in today's schools challenge educators to examine not whether, but how they will respond to their needs.

REFERENCES

Merchant, B. (1999). Ghosts in the classroom: Unavoidable casualties of a principal's commitment to the status quo. *Journal for the Education of Students Placed at Risk, 4* (2), 153–171.

National Center for Education Statistics. (1996). The Conditions of Education, 1996. Indicator 43 [Online]. Available: http://nces.ed.gov/pubsold/ce96/c9643a01.html [1999, May 22].

National Center for Education Statistics (1997a). The Conditions of Education, 1997. Indicator 45 [Online]. Available: http://nces.ed.gov/pubs/ce/c9745a01.html [1999, May 22].

National Center for Education Statistics (1997b). *Digest of Education Statistics, 1997* [Online]. Available: http://nces.ed.gov/pubs/digest97/d97t069.html [1999, May 22].

United States Bureau of the Census. (1998). *Statistical Abstract of the United States: 1998.* Washington, DC: United States Bureau of the Census.

U.S. Department of Education. National Center for Education Statistics. (1996). *Schools and staffing in the United States: A statistical profile, 1993–1994.* NCES 96-124, by R. R. Henke, S. P. Choy, S. Geis, & S. P. Broughman. Washington, DC: author.

6

THE POWER OF THE POLITICAL: BEYOND PROFESSIONALISM IN INTEGRATING PROGRAMS FOR CHILDREN

Carolyn D. Herrington
Florida State University

INTRODUCTION

At the end of the last century, stimulated by attempts to professionalize school administration and by urban educational reform movements, school systems became separate and increasingly isolated from the political and social give-and-take of community life and from the social structures, such as the family, the neighborhoods, and the local governments, of the children they were schooling. While this *splendid isolation* in many ways served the educational system well for most of the 20th century, it is now increasingly apparent that in the 21st century, this separation model is no longer powerful enough. To forge the collective will and marshal the institutional resources necessary to prepare the children of the country for the next century requires new formulations.

This chapter provides an overview and critique of the historical relationships, political and professional, between school systems and other systems and agencies that serve children. It investigates new roles for educational administrators in assuming political leadership and administrative responsibility for innovative programming on behalf of all children in a school's community.

The high level of material stress experienced in many American families and the high level of social stress experienced in ever larger numbers of American families suggests a need for a more focused, sensitive, and intense response from communities, professionals, and institutions charged with educating children and supporting their families. Yet the institutional and professional structures of schooling and other children-serving agencies have pressed in the opposite direction over the last century.

Recently, policy analysts and child advocates have questioned the need for closer linkages between the educational sector and the other sectors serving children and their families (Center for the Future of Children, 1992; Kirst, 1991; Leiderman, Reveal, Rosewater, Stephens, & Wolf, 1991). In particular, some have proposed placing social and health services in the school system, arguing that the sheer size and monolithic structure of public schooling make it one of the most stable and dependable institutions acting on behalf of children. According to this line of thinking, the school system can play the role of the core or home for a broad array of services because it is large, relatively well funded, and stable, with an extensive network of personnel and facilities throughout virtually all communities with children. On the other hand, critics charge that precisely because of its large size and bureaucratic structure, the public school system lacks accountability for its actions and flexibility to respond to changing conditions. Its independent and dedicated funding sources and political autonomy from other governments and community agencies mean that it has neither the professional culture nor political incentives to collaborate.

To some degree, this is a reprise of an equally vigorous and still inconclusive debate that energized child advocates and public policy students in the 1960s (Katz, 1989; Lazar, 1991; Trattner, 1989). There are many similarities but also important distinctions. The central issue of child poverty was highlighted by the incongruity of a general prosperity virtually unequaled in human experience. How could a country of such affluence tolerate such high levels of child poverty? There was a relatively broad consensus that it fell to government to take responsibility and, therefore, actions should be taken against the most egregious manifestations of material want. Today, the consensus is still broad on the degree of the problem but less unified on the means governments should employ to address the problems. There is also a greater sense of urgency fueled by a spread of many problems to the middle class such as drug abuse, unstable home life, insecure employment, and a fragile system of health services. The challenges facing educational administrators are, if anything, more complex and community consensus more elusive.

Furthermore, even those most optimistic about the United States economy at the turn of the century raise concerns. Even though the country is riding the crest of an economic boom unparalleled in its strength and in its tenure in recent memory, and the rising tide is clearly benefiting low-income communities by contributing to higher employment rates, lower crime, and fewer drugs, schools have not been excused. Some voices argue that the real want in this country may be less material than cultural and spiritual (see Finn, 1991; Katz, 1989; Pipher, 1996; Schorr, 1997). Educators are being drawn into an increasingly acrimonious debate about "character" and the role schools may play in developing character traits presumably requisite to a civil society and a healthy polity.

Despite the lack of support from an increasingly fractured educational community, weak local communities, and an insufficient intergovernmental support structure, the role of school administrators has been expanding incrementally to include responsibility for children' well-being in areas other than that of formal schooling. New roles and responsibilities have been added to school and it has fallen to school administration to implement these changes in the schooling environment. These changes in some cases are minor but, in others, raise fundamental challenges to conventional formulations of school administrators, the relationship between schooling and society, and accepted dogma about good practice (see Mitchell & Cunningham, 1990; Murphy, 1992).

From all of this, the question that school administrators must address is what is the role of educational administrators given the context of greater demands from society to meet a broad array of needs of children and families. The formulation of the school administrator as the chief administrator has been falling apart since the 1960s, replaced by the formulation of a professional working within a broad range of discretion. Yet, as this century ends, this formulation, too, is called into question. In a post-industrial, information-intensive society, where hyper-change and the expectations of hyper-responsiveness hold sway, conventional conceptions of leadership, administrative and political management, and schooling are vulnerable to charges of insularity and lethargy.

INDUSTRIALIZATION AND CHANGING ROLES
OF HUMAN SERVICES PROVIDERS

New Economy

The current set of relationships between society and schooling are the result of economic, sociodemographic, and educational changes that swept through the United States at the end of the 19th century (see Beeghley & Dwyer, 1989; Cremin, 1989; Peterson, 1985; Tyack, 1992, 1974). These changes were driven, in large part, by the economic transformation of the United States from a largely agrarian, family-centered, craft-focused economy to one fueled by larger units of production outside of the home and owned by proprietors. New factories, plants, and industries, and accompanying retail establishments, profoundly changed the relationships among families, neighborhood, and schooling. Where families had been units of production, they became consumers of production. Where individuals had worked at home, in crafts learned informally from older practitioners, more formal training in larger and more depersonalized workplaces became the norm. These economic transformations in turn propelled sociological and demographic changes. Families became smaller. Members worked less with one another and encounters with strangers were more frequent. The growing economy demanded large labor forces resulting in the largest migration of people the world had ever seen, primarily from southern and eastern Europe to the United States. Most of these people were from agrarian societies, did not speak English. and were illiterate in their own languages.

New Organizations

Schooling was likewise transformed. Enormous growth in population created the need to rapidly expand the existing schools. The new industrial order required workers with more advanced training and with different attitudes toward work. The large numbers of immigrants added a socializing, or "Americanizing" function to schools. The industrialization process that was propelling these new requirements also offered a new managerial model to meet them. The industrial workplace offered several principles that could be applied to restructure schooling to meet the new demands for growth in student enrollment, for training opportunities for employees of the new workplace, and for socializing new immigrants. These could be applied relatively rapidly and efficiently.

Borrowed from the industrial economy were the values of control, division of labor and separation of the workforce into managers and workers, and quality assurance. As organizations, the public school systems developed into highly centralized, rationalized, and bureaucratized service delivery systems, dividing tasks, valuing control and efficiency, and assuring quality through supervision.

As political systems, the challenge was even greater. Unlike industry, schooling was a public sector enterprise responsible to citizens and their elected leaders. Again drawing upon analogies from the private sector, democratic control was maintained but buffered from other political forces through the separation of funding sources (property tax), leadership (school boards), and electoral cycles from other political influences in the community. Administrative challenges were not as difficult to address. Because the political structure assured a limited but still democratic control of public schools through elected leadership (school boards), administrative responsibilities could be handled through separating leadership and operational functions. By removing day-to-day responsibilities for running the schools from school boards and centralizing responsibility for operations under a chief administrative officer (the superintendent), and through him or her the other school leaders (notably principals), a centralized, and arguably more efficient system was created that was capable of responding to the immense challenges of the new era: growth in student enrollment, higher training requirements, and socialization of new immigrants.

New Roles

The requirements of personnel called upon to work in this new organization—large, complex, and rationalized—changed along with the organizations (Beeghley & Dwyer, 1989; James, 1993; Lazar, 1991; Leiderman et al., 1991). The new employees—both managerial and instructional—were a hybrid of bureaucratic and professionally oriented workers. Both administrative and instructional staff retained large areas of discretion that they previously held when school systems were small and policies highly personalistic, and in that degree, could be considered professional. But, they remained employees of a large organization, were excluded from overall policy development, and were supervised by superiors, not by peers. Regulations became more extensive through credentialing, licensing, and formal policies. This hybrid of the professional and the bureaucratic proved highly resilient and, throughout the first half of the 20th century, was not challenged (March, 1978; Murphy, 1990).

This same rationalizing, bureaucratizing, and enlarging of organizational forces were holding sway in the other human services. Particularly of interest to educators are the other areas that served children. Up until earlier in the 20th century, there were essentially three simply defined human services and three groups of largely unregulated groups of providers of these services. In addition to educators, there were health care providers and social service workers. These other two underwent similar professionalization, which resulted in a multiplying number of specialists with increasingly narrow focuses. The field of social work had its origins in individual philanthropy, often genteel women volunteers, who were paid nothing, and where good intentions substituted for skills and knowledge. As home visits became ineffective and unsafe in the rapidly urbanizing cities, social service sites were created—the settlement house. A number of different services could thus be offered in one site—counseling and recreation, adult education and day care, emergency shelter, medical and legal services, job leads, and advocacy. Quickly, volunteers and the newly emerging paid staff became assigned to and required special training in the distinct areas. Similarly, the informal apprenticeship of physicians, surgeons, and nurses, requiring only certificates by their mentors, gave way to a tightly controlled system of elite medical schools controlling entrance to the profession and instituting certification and licensure process for themselves and other heath care professionals. In all three cases, educational requirements doubled and tripled in a matter of decades and broad areas of service became whittled down to an array of specialties. Hence, the emergence of the pediatric neuro-otlaryngologist, the adolescent mental health therapist, and the high school English teacher (Lazar, 1991).

Role Differentiation Within Schools

An array of professional differentiation also developed within schools to meet the social and health needs of children (Herrington & Lazar, 1999). Three patterns of inclusion of the other human services have been pursued by schools: (1) schools subsume the other professions by appointing teachers to carry out the functions; (2) schools directly employ other professionals to carry out these functions; or (3) schools provide the site and offices in which other agencies offer their services. Historically, schools have preferred the first option. They have preferred to co-opt the other professions rather than cooperate. In most states, schools have acquired exemptions from requirements of licensure or certification for their own employees that practice in other professional areas. As a result, rather than invite other agencies in, they either appoint teachers to carry out the function, or, in conjunction with the teacher colleges, create their own professional training programs for psychologists, social workers (counselors), and health educators. Even though this is often more expensive than hiring certified or licensed personnel in these areas, it provides the schools with greater control and maintains their monopoly on school-based programs and facilities.

Professionalism has been the target of much praise and much blame for the fragmentation in service provider roles, (Kimball, 1992; Kirst, 1991). The new organizations valued specialization. Its managers relied on expertise for the determination of what to do and on peers to determine if it had been done well. Absent from this formulization was the knowledge, understanding, and desires of the people to whom it was being done. The strengths (and the weaknesses) of professionalism relied on the knowledge gap between the lay and the initiated. There is no question that the 20th century greatly benefited from expert knowledge coupled with application to problems.

Professionalism has traditionally been defined in terms of an association of individuals possessing valid and useful knowledge in certain areas and incorporating an ethic of service (Freidson, 1983; Kimball, 1992). The autonomy in practice that has accompanied the expertise has been a hallmark of professionalism. But its growth, success, and institutionalization throughout the 20th century, particularly as abetted by increasingly specialized preparation programs, governmental licensure and certification, and peer evaluation, has also led to charges of abuse and to bureaucratic insularity. Increasingly, professionalism is charged with being a means to translate one set of scarce resources—specialized knowledge and skills—into another—social and economic rewards. These include charges of legitimating the deliberate manipulation of expertise to make specialized knowledge artificial and abstruse in order to intimidate and exclude others (Kimball, 1992).

Throughout the early years of the 20th century, one by one, the child-serving professions, health care, social work, and education, have been submitted to this professionalizing routine with remarkable increases in quality, standards, and effectiveness. These professions have experienced significant development in the professionalization of their fields in this century, including lengthened periods of preparation, restrictions on who may enter the profession, increasing bureaucratization of the practice site, and unprecedented growth in the knowledge base and the technology of practice.

NEED FOR NEW ORGANIZATIONAL AND
PROFESSIONAL MODELS

Today, however, the strategies of organizational strength and professional practice are under considerable challenge. Although there are a host of reasons, the two dominant ones are clear. One, the sheer magnitude and diversity of services needed by children have overwhelmed schools' and other agencies' capacity to absorb them. Second, the movement within the human services field toward positing the family as the unit of service has made it increasingly difficult for one agency to remain aloof from the rest of the service community. The weakening of society and the compartmentalization of professional providers creates a greater need for educational administrators to take leadership roles in addressing the issues of child wellbeing. These factors also make the obstacles to successful action all the more daunting. The challenges facing educational administrators today are intimidating and the infrastructures to work within are weak. Healthy community and family structures supported by extended families, caring neighborhoods, and religious institutions are weak and divided and, in many cases, absent. As society has become more complex, community life more secular, and individuals more mobile, neighborhoods have become less vital and neighbors more isolated. The capacity of local governmental and voluntary communities has been seriously challenged. As community-level actors come under increased pressure to strengthen their services on behalf of children and their families, the actors turn to the local schools. Their size, their facilities, their expertise, and influence over children posit them as necessary allies.

But the bureaucratic nature of school organizations and the professional values of adherence to professional norms of what constitutes best practice combine to blunt school actors desire and ability to respond to conditions they cannot control and lack the professional body of knowledge to draw upon.

WHAT RECENT EXPERIENCES CAN TEACH US

Evidence from existing research on innovative, integrated services programming is compiled to help focus on the capacities and limitations of public school systems and the professionals that administer them. Three innovative programs, selected because they attempt to engage school leaders more deeply with the community and with other service providers in other areas, are described. The programs represent, along a continuum of deeper engagement, attempts to use the schooling infrastructure in communities, professionals, facilities, management information services, and others, to further community development or simply to increase access to health care or other social service for children. The degree of success in creating more effective and more efficient service delivery systems for children by utilizing existing school resources and personnel varies considerably and reveals much about the insufficiency of the current formulations of educational administration. It may also provide direction for more promising avenues in the future.

The first is an overview of the findings from a survey of educational administrators who were involved in modest attempts to render access for children and their families to other social or health care services through housing the programming and personnel on the school campus. The second is drawn from a book-length study of a program that requires schools and public health units to work cooperatively in neighborhoods with large percentages of at-risk children. The third is an overview of some learnings to emerge from one of the most ambitious and generously funded efforts to date to unite all major community stakeholders in a long-term initiative to improve the condition of children in troubled communities. When advanced along a continuum, these findings suggest the strength of the educational delivery system in serving as a house for additional services, particularly if it does not require reconfiguring existing professional or institutional norms. But, it also reveals a certain intransigence when solutions are not ready-made but must be forged out of the life of the community itself.

Housing Other Programs for Children at Schools

A series of interviews were conducted in 1993–1994 (Herrington, 1994) among school principals and superintendents in one state involved in integrated services programming. Another agency places its personnel and programs on a school campus but the school does not hire, train, or accept responsibilities for the professionals delivering the services. The agencies most frequently involved were public health agencies and local police or sheriff departments. The professionals most frequently found were registered nurses and police officers or sheriff deputies. Others, however, others included physicians, social service workers, drug abuse counselors, and employment support personnel. Although no outcome data are available on program outcomes to assess impacts on children or families, the programs were selected because they were generally considered to be successful (see Herrington, 1995). A set of questions was posed to the school- and district-level administrators about the accommodations and problems associated with the presence of nondistrict employees and professionals from other service areas on campus. Notable about their response is their affirmation that there was no clash between the different professionals or the agencies with which the schools worked. The educational administrators interviewed reported that the programming was offered on campus without any significant organizational malaccomodations, professional resistance, or tensions over goals. Further probing revealed that it was precisely the parallel nature of the programming that resulted in its smooth insertion. The new programs and the personnel that delivered the services did not challenge the professional culture and norms of educators, did not require modification of the standard operation procedures of the schools, or threaten the existing accommodations among the core school personnel, that is, the instructional staff and the school leadership. This view is consonant with research that has shown schools to be remarkably adaptable to the addition of new duties, functions, and responsibilities as long as fundamental accommodations are not challenged (Wirt & Kirst, 1997). This new program offered educational professionals the opportunity to hand-off noninstructional problems to the professionals from the other agencies, which was greatly appreciated by the school staff. The administrators reported that teachers were pleased to be able to drop what were seen as noneducational problems (drugs, pregnancies, truancy) in the lap of another responsible agent (registered nurses, police officers, social workers, etc.) who presumably had the role, authority, preparation, and expertise to deal with them. The administrators also reported that the program required little additional supervision or monitoring on their part. The two most common programs in the schools, public health and law enforcement, seemed particularly amenable to inclusion within schools precisely because they occupied distinct professional niches not related to education.

In this example, educational administrators were not required to rethink their organizational objectives or structures or deal with any new constituencies. They were simply required to manage an additional office that already had its own objectives, personnel, and organizational structure. Technical issues related to logistics were easily addressed and no professional or political issues were raised.

School-Based Health Services

A second model was the inclusion of noneducational programming by the school system with school district employees. A book-length study (Emihovich & Herrington, 1997) was undertaken on a series of high schools in poorly resourced communities that suffered from high infant mortality, low birth weight babies, and high incidences of teenage childbearing. The schools were provided with additional resources to hire school nurses and other health care professionals to deal with students engaged in a host of at-risk behaviors. This program differs from the previous one in two ways. One, the school system is administratively involved with the programs. The services vary considerably by local choice and are delivered by district employees who report either to district health coordinators or to building-level administrators. Most tellingly, the programming is targeted to a social problem, which deals with youth risk behavior, particularly too-early sexual activity, for which there is no community consensus on appropriate preventive strategies. The local school administrators were given considerable discretion in how they choose to use the funds and the personnel to employ. Even though it was well understood that the students' risk-taking behaviors stemmed from a complex mixture of social, cultural and economic forces, however, educators and the other health care professionals seemed reluctant to engage lay people, community leadership, or the parents and families of the students in forming programmatic approaches. They appeared reluctant to reach beyond their respective professional areas and institutional boundaries or to engage with other community and family members whose influence in the students' lives was so great. Despite the flexibility deliberately built into the program to allow for customized, tailored responses in different communities, little exploitation of the flexibility was found. Responses remained constrained within narrow conceptions of professional best practice. Seeking out community-based or community-legitimated solutions was not found.

New Futures Program

Perhaps the most carefully crafted, generously funded, and most closely documented attempt to improve outcomes for children through a community-wide approach, was the New Futures initiative funded by the Annie E. Casey Foundation in 1987 (Walsh, n.d.). Offering $10 million over 5 years to 10 cities, it attempted to experiment with collaborative, comprehensive, public–private approaches to the multiple problems of "at-risk" children. Eschewing the more modest and incremental approaches characteristic of other community improvement initiatives, the New Futures venture set out to use the strategies of strong political leadership, interagency collaboration, case management, and other comprehensive strategies to reduce teenage pregnancy and school dropout rates and to improve student achievement and youth employment rates in a 5-year period. Its planners drew upon the best of thinking to craft a very inclusive design and to define the problems and the ways to measure success. Still, the projects fell far short of the designers hopes and failed to achieve measurable improvements in the social health of the children of the communities.

Of the many lessons learned, one that is particular germane to the efficacy of professional administration within schools is the necessity of educational administrators becoming competent community leaders and adept in the skills of political leadership. Although the educational system was seen as a key component of any successful strategy, the educational systems seemed particularly intransigent in cooperating with other service providers. One of the superintendents summed his learning from the venture.

> If the school system is ever going to change, it's going to come from outside community pressure, not from an internal realization that we need reform. . . . There are not enough organized, well-informed groups in poor communities that can go up against these big public systems with facts and strategies. Middle- and upper-income communities do that—they make their schools work, for instance, because they have the kind of knowledge, the resources and the time to go toe-to-toe with these systems. (Walsh, n.d., p. 13.)

A conclusion reached by many of the participants was that the solutions lie less in the services for children and more in the development of communities that are authentic and self-defining, communities that build on the indigenous wisdom, strengths, and values of the community members themselves.

CONCLUSION

A look back at child-serving organizations in the 20th century reminds us that governmental and nongovernmental, educational, and other informal organizations for children are interconnected agents of socialization with similar organizational and professional norms. James (1993) even questions the presumption that community-based agencies are more responsive to community needs than large organizations such as school systems. He notes that they both share organizational norms of control and are motivated by fear.

> Out-of-school organizations cannot be treated merely as alternatives of dysfunctional schooling practices. They are part of a combined reality with mainstream organizations . . . to help young people find some place for themselves in family, community, work place and public bureaucracies, youth organizations must re-examine the highly problematic but powerful nexus of institutional rules that supports or impede the growth of particular types of organization. (p. 191)

This suggests that the limitations of educational administrators to affect broad-based changes on behalf of children are not just questions of size and bureaucratic inflexibility. They may speak to a failure to openly acknowledge that certain religious or ideological beliefs, cultural norms, family practices, and social arrangements are not amenable to professional analyses. What is needed is a deeper formulation of professional discretion to acknowledge respect for communities and a willingness to concede moral, religious, and ideological diversity. There must be a willingness to concede moral authority to others and to support communities by eliciting from them programmatic content and strategies. Professionalism must be redefined such that such concessions are not perceived to be an abdication of professional standards, competence, or responsibility but a redefinition and a rethinking of their fundamental sources of authority—legal and moral. Sarason (1995), in an essay on the role of parents in schooling, insists upon the radicality of the notion that parents' values must be a factor in determining institutional policy and practice. He formulates the simple political principle, "When you are going to be affected, directly or indirectly, by a decision, you should stand in some relationship to the decision-making process" (p. 5). Sarason underscores that this is not a technical point, but constitutes an absolute redistribution of power based on a shift in the source of legitimacy.

Conditions of children facing educational administrators today are daunting. Educators, as well as health care professionals and social service workers, struggle to balance a control function with a service mandate, often at odds with one another. Successfully attacking poor conditions for children often require multiple partnerships and multifocused strategies. But the bureaucracies that administrators function in continue with hierarchical and across-the-board responses. Far too often, bureaucracies continue to function as if they had a monolithic purchase over the communities they serve, ignoring the diversity of opinions within the community or the plethora of other resources, small and large, also present in the community. Health and education administrators continue to be dominated by the direct-service orientation, where human behavior is stressed to the relative neglect of theories of social behavior.

Many issues confronted in dealing more broadly with the condition of children deal with values and legitimacy and are ultimately political in nature. Professionals are often loath to get involved in them. The barriers that professionals have erected around themselves—in the name of quality and expertise—distance them from those they are committed to serve. The disdain of things political makes them ill equipped to deal with the value-laden realities that shape the lives of children, families, and communities.

REFERENCES

Beeghley, L., & Dwyer, J. W. (1989). Social structure and the rate of divorce. In J. A. Holstein & G. Miller (Eds.), *Perspectives on social problems, Vol. 1* (pp. 56–84). Greenwich, CT: JAI Press.

Center for the Future of Children. (1992). *School linked services.* Los Altos, CA: Author.

Cremin, L. A. (1988). *American education: The metropolitan experience 1876–1980.* New York: Harper & Row.

Emihovich, C., & Herrington, C. D. (1997). *Sex, kids and politics. Health services in schools.* New York: Columbia University Press.

Finn, C. (1991). *We must take charge: Our schools and our future.* New York: Free Press.

Freidson, E. (1983). The theory of professions: State of the art. In R. Dingle & P. Lewis (Eds.), *The sociology of the professions: Lawyers, doctors and others.* London: Macmillan Press.

Herrington, C. D. (1994, August). Schools as intergovernmental partners: Administrator perceptions of expanded programming for children. *Educational Administration Quarterly, 30*(3), 301–323.

Herrington, C. D., & Lazar, I. (1999). Evaluating integrated children's services: The politics of research on collaborative education and social service research. In B. S. Cooper & E. V. Randall (Eds.), *Accuracy or advocacy: The politics of research in education* (pp. 424–452). Thousand Oaks, CA: Corwin Press.

James, T. (1993). The winnowing of organizations. In S. B. Heath & M. W. McLaughlin (Eds.), *Identity and inner-city youth: Beyond ethnicity and gender.* New York: Teachers College Press.

Katz, M. (1989). *The undeserving poor: From the war on poverty to the war on welfare.* New York: Pantheon.

Kimball, B. A. (1992). *The "True Professional Ideal" in America*. Cambridge, MA: Blackwell.

Kirst, M. W. (1991). Improving children's services: Overcoming barriers, creating new opportunities. *Phi Delta Kappan, 72*, 615–618.

Lazar, I. (1991). *Notes on a framework for care*. Unpublished paper. Ithaca, NY: Author.

Leiderman, S., Reveal, E. C., Rosewater, A., Stephens, S. A., & Wolf, W. C. (1991). *The children's initiative: Making systems work*. A design document for the Pew Charitable Trusts. Philadelphia, PA: Center for Assessment & Policy Development.

March, J. G. (1978, February). American public school administration: A short analysis. *School Review, 86*, 217–250.

Mitchell, B., & Cunningham, L. L. (Eds.). (1990). *Educational leadership and changing contexts of families, communities, and schools* (Eighty-ninth NSSE yearbook, Part II). Chicago: University of Chicago Press.

Murphy, J. (1992). *The landscape of leadership preparation: Reframing the education of school administrators*. Newbury Park, CA: Corwin Press.

Murphy, J. (1990). Principal instructional leadership. In L. S. Lotto & P. W. Thurston (Eds.), *Advances in educational administration: Changing perspectives on the school*. (Vol. 1, Part B, pp. 163–200). Greenwich, CT: JAI Press.

Peterson, P. E. (1985). *The politics of school reform, 1870–1940*. Chicago: University of Chicago Press.

Pipher, M. (1996). *The shelter of each other: rebuilding our families*. New York: Random House.

Sarason, S. B. (1995). *Parental involvement and the political principle*. San Francisco: Jossey-Bass.

Schorr, L. B. (1997). *Common purpose: Strengthening families and neighborhoods to rebuild America*. New York: Doubleday.

Trattner, W. I. (1989). *From poor law to welfare state*. New York: Collier Macmillan Publishers.

Tyack, D. B. (1974). *The one best system: A history of American urban education*. Cambridge: Harvard University Press.

Tyack, D. B. (1992, Spring). Health and social services in public schools: Historical perspectives. *The future of children, 2*(1), 19–31.

Walsh, J. (n.d.). *The eye of the storm: Ten years on the front lines of new futures*. A report prepared for the Annie E. Casey Foundation, Baltimore, MD.

Wirt, F. M., & Kirst, M. (1997). *The political dynamics of American education*. Berkeley: McCutchan Publishing Corporation.

part III
School Reform: National and Local Dynamic

7

NATIONAL STANDARDS IN LOCAL CONTEXT: A PHILOSOPHICAL AND POLICY ANALYSIS

Barry Bull
Indiana University

The educational system in the United States is notoriously decentralized, especially in comparison with those of most industrialized nations of Europe and Asia. The United States Constitution leaves education as a function of state governments, and in all states other than Hawaii, state educational authority is further delegated to school districts. As a result, federal education policy has been largely a matter of incentives and persuasion rather that mandates, with the notable exception of the federal courts' enforcement of constitutional rights on states and localities.

In elementary and secondary education, policy initially took the form of funding for particular categorical programs, such as vocational and compensatory education. By providing money for particular educational activities, federal policy makers hoped to encourage state legislatures and school districts to revise their educational policies and practices. But money alone has rarely been the exclusive federal strategy for changing the educational system. Such incentives have consistently been accompanied by rhetorical efforts to create a popular demand for specific educational changes, usually capitalizing on public anxieties about prevailing national problems. Thus, federal incentive programs were usually represented as part of a larger effort to achieve a variety of national goals, ranging from political stability and industrial development to national defense and the elimination of poverty.

During the Reagan administration, this hortatory strategy of federal education reform became a high art, particularly under Secretary of Education William Bennett. In fact, given the Reagan administration's attempts to restrain federal education spending, persuasion effectively displaced funding as the primary federal approach to education reform. In 1983, *A Nation at Risk*, the school reform report of the federal government's National Commission for Excellence in Education, connected the American public's worries about the nation's economic future to the performance of its schools (National Commission for Excellence in Education, 1983). As a result, the federal government urged governors and other state officials to change state education policies in a variety of ways—through, for instance, higher stakes state testing of students and more stringent certification of teachers. During the 1980s, state after state adopted some portion of these recommended policy changes, often with significant political fanfare but with little federal assistance.

Despite this state activism, and despite a general recovery of American economic strength, the public and political leaders continued to be concerned about the performance of schools and their students. The most frequently predicted source of failure of the 1980s reforms, namely local resistance, simply did not occur. Berman and McLaughlin (1975–1978) conducted landmark Rand change-agent studies in the 1970s. Results suggested that many previous federal efforts to stimulate local change in education foundered for lack of local political will to act. Nevertheless, studies of state and local response to the 1980s school reforms showed that school districts and schools often went beyond what federal guidelines and state laws required (Fuhrman, Clune, & Elmore, 1988).

In the early 1990s, the Clinton administration seemed to have three related explanations for the failure of federal exhortations on behalf of school reform. First, the states did not adopt a coherent approach to school change. Second, without federal incentives, established state political structures resisted various critical elements of reform that needed to be included in a more coherent approach. Third, school systems more often than not lacked the capacity to implement the changes needed to achieve real reform. To correct these problems, Goals 2000 (1994) urged states to develop their own systemic educational standards and gave them federal funding to do so. It also included an additional national education goal that called for all teachers to "have access to programs for the continued improvement of their professional skills" (Section 102, 4A) and provided funding to states to implement professional development programs that were to be aligned with the standards they developed.

In President Clinton's second term, however, there began to be some disenchantment with the initial Goals 2000 strategy. The state standards developed with federal assistance were often lacking in rigor and enforcement. As a result, the Clinton administration began to urge the development and adoption of national educational standards and to use Title I, by far the largest program of federal aid to education, to impose such standards and related school reform programs on individual schools.

The logic that is leading the United States toward national standards is apparently impeccable. The nation's school system will not be able to improve the performance of its students as long as the visions that govern it pull teachers, schools, and districts in dozens of incompatible directions. Moreover, these disparate visions of schooling militate against the achievement of equal educational opportunity for the nation's children. The fragmentation of decisionmaking about the schools in fifty state legislatures and thousands of local districts, however, makes it unlikely that a coherent vision of schooling will emerge on its own. Thus, it becomes imperative that the national government sponsor an effort to develop national standards that can guide these various education authorities in a common direction. Beyond the articulation of these standards, it is crucial for the federal government to use its considerable ideological and fiscal resources to persuade the states and localities to join in a concerted effort to adopt and implement these standards.

In this chapter however, it is argued that this line of reasoning makes three crucial mistakes, all of which are related to the capacity of schools to enable children to learn. The logic of national standards represents a particular account of political will rather than capacity to promote student learning as the primary barrier to school improvement. First, this account of the proper conduct of public schooling is based upon a problematic theory of democracy, a theory to which a more justifiable alternative is available. Second, the way in which the movement for national standards attends to schools' capacity to systematically promote learning misrepresents and misunderstands what that capacity means and how it is achieved. Third, the national standards movement assumes, erroneously, that equality of opportunity is achieved when students attend schools that follow clear and predictable standards rather than schools with a robust capacity to promote student learning. In preparation for these arguments it is necessary to understand how the proponents of national standards understand them and think about their implementation.

WHAT NATIONAL STANDARDS ARE AND HOW THEY ARE SUPPOSED TO WORK

Coherence is a central theme of the national standards movement. Specifically, the inability of the school system to produce consistent effects on student achievement is taken to imply that the country needs a common agreement about those effects and how to produce them. That inability is thought to have two primary consequences. First, it causes the system as a whole to produce competing results that, as often as not, cancel each other out. On a small scale, if the teachers in a single school fail to define their goals and instructional strategies in ways that complement and build upon one another, their students may try to learn many things in many different ways, but they are unlikely to learn anything rigorously or in depth. On a large scale, even if individual teachers and schools succeed in teaching their students what their particular goals and procedures call for, such vastly disparate results are not likely to match the needs of the nation's economic, political, or social systems. Second, such diverse and inconsistent results are likely to disadvantage certain children educationally and socially. To the extent that the teachers and schools of minority or poor students have different aims or use different procedures than those of nonminority or nonpoor students, those students are likely to have systematically different opportunities as adults.

The coherence implied by national standards extends in two directions. On the one hand, such standards are to be internally consistent. Systemic reformers call for the development of standards of three different kinds—standards for outcomes, curriculum, and resources (Smith & O'Day, 1991). Curriculum frameworks should ensure that the material taught to students will most effectively allow them to achieve the outcomes standards. Resources available to schools and teachers (prescribed in what are often called opportunity-to-learn standards) should most effectively support the curriculum to be taught and thus, students' efforts to meet the outcome standards.

On the other hand, the standards are to be consistent with the policies and procedures whereby they are implemented. Such policy alignment, as it is called, requires, for example, that the accountability measure applied to students and schools reflect the outcomes to be achieved, the curriculum to be taught, and the resources to be provided. Policies that are consistent with the achievement of the standards should be enacted; those irrelevant to the standards should be repealed. Admittedly, there is considerable controversy over just which policies align best with various standards. For instance, some reformers prefer heightened rationalization of the regulation of public schools as most likely to produce coherent implementation of the standards. Others call for increased parental choice among schools as the most likely element to encourage schools to meet these standards (Clune, 1993). Nevertheless, the idea of policy alignment seems basic to the national standards movement.

It should be clear that this focus on coherence is intended to address a particular conception of the problem of political will in the development and implementation of education reform policy. This approach diagnoses the primary shortcoming of the system as one in which disparate goals and preferences among political interest groups, politicians, and communities convey different and conflicting expectations to teachers, administrators, and students. Under these circumstances, teachers and administrators who genuinely wish to comply with these expectations are often wasting their energies in trying to meet excessive, conflicting, and changing demands. Beyond that, these incoherent expectations unintentionally permit some teachers and administrators to pick and choose among the various demands made on them based on their own interest and preferences. Thus, the *incoherence* of standards and policy causes the problem of will to occur at two levels, at the level of basic political authority over the aims and procedures of the education system and at the level of implementation and service delivery. National agreement about standards addresses the problem of political will at the level of basic authority.

Alignment of policy with the standards reduces the scope for street-level bureaucrats (that is, teachers, principals, and other school employees) to evade legitimate political authority over education.

DEMOCRACY AND POLITICAL WILL

Democratic political theory has taken a wide variety of forms over the past 250 years. Two forms are of particular relevance to this analysis—those based on the work of Jean Jacques Rousseau and those based on the work of John Dewey.

For Rousseau (1762/1950), one of the founding theorists of modern democratic philosophy, democracy is the emergence, articulation, and political ascendancy of what he called the general will. Rousseau distinguished the general will from any particular intentions and desires that emerge from social circumstance, notably the differential interests that arise from social stratification. It represents the permanent and common interests of human beings in social relationship with one another, as opposed to the competing and superficial interests that arise from specific forms of hierarchical social organization. A political order is truly democratic (and thus, morally justified) when it permits this general will to be expressed and to be the authoritative source of public policy. On this account, the constitution of a democratic society has two tasks. First, it must permit the articulation of a democratic political will that is uncontaminated by parochial interests. Second, it must make this general political will the effective source of the policies adopted and enforced in the society.

Later developments of this strand of democratic theory, which I call democratic authoritarianism, rejected some elements of Rousseau's original vision but maintained others. Hegel (1821/1942), for instance, doubted whether the general will was already available in the current constitution of the world but suggested, rather, that it was gradually emerging through human history. Marx (Marx & Engels, 1848/1972), in a variation on Hegel, asserted that the historically inevitable version of political will was actually expressed by the interests of a particular social and economic class. Twentieth-century interest group theorists maintained that democratic will was an aggregation of the interests of particular groups of citizens constructed through particular decision-making processes (Dahl, 1971).

As important as the differences among these variations may be, they all maintain an allegiance to one of Rousseau's major premises, that is, however the appropriate version of political will is to be identified, a democratic government is to have the authority to enforce that will on all citizens through policies and procedures that are aligned with it. The political theory that stands behind the current movement toward national educational standards seems clearly committed to this central premise of democratic authoritarianism.

On the one hand, this movement is committed to the idea that a society-wide agreement about such standards is both possible and valuable. In other words, a society's democratic will has been fully articulated only when a coherent expression of the polity's intentions has emerged about the goals of the society and the appropriate means of achieving them. To be sure, the content of this will may be subject to reformulation over time, but a society without such an expression of will, however revisable it may be, is not truly democratic because it permits contradictory aspirations on the part of its citizens.

On the other hand, the standards movement is committed to the alignment of political authority with this coherent expression of democratic will. A society without such an alignment of authority to the polity's will is not fully democratic because it permits the exercise of public authority in ways that are opposed to the democratic will. In other words, unless the exercises of public authority is governed entirely by the express will of the polity, public authority can, at times, be used for what can only be private purposes. To be sure, a democratic society on this account can include a sphere of private purposes and actions, but the polity must be able to define the scope of this private sphere, and within that sphere the instrumentalities of public authority may not be applied.

The criticisms of this strand of democratic theory have been many and various, but one is especially relevant to this analysis. In assigning central importance to the development and implementation of a coherent political will, democratic authoritarianism rests on basic premise of moral theory formulated by Kant (1785/1964), that is, that good actions are those and only those done with a good will. One primary objection to democratic authoritarianism is that this premise neglects the consequences of policies. In policy analysis, this objection is related to what is frequently called the doctrine of *unintended consequences*, that is, public policies can and often do have results that were not envisioned by policy makers and that often vitiate those policies despite the good intentions with which they were enacted. In the context of national standards, this doctrine maintains that many teachers may not have the capacity to enable their students to meet such standards, either because they lack the requisite understanding of subject matter or the pedagogical skills to permit their students to master that subject matter. As a result, a number of unfortunate consequences may follow, such as the disadvantage of some students whose teachers are particularly incompetent in this regard. The usual response to the doctrine of unintended consequences in this context is that the resource standards are supposed to prevent such circumstances from arising. These opportunity-to-learn standards, when implemented, should ensure that the capacity of teachers has been realigned to the outcome standards so the inequalities in student learning, for example, will be avoided. In other words, teacher incompetence can be remedied, and the unintended consequences can be prevented.

This objection runs deeper than this standard version of the doctrine of unintended consequences, however, and, therefore, the usual response is not adequate to meet it. Even if the intentions of the democratic will are carried out by means of the alignment of capacity with political will, the world has become a different place that it was when the democratic will was formulated originally. In particular, it has become a world inhabited by people with changed capacities. Also, there is no guarantee, indeed, there can be no guarantee, that the intended consequences, even if successfully achieved, will be experienced as good from the vantage point of those with these changed capacities.

A hypothetical example will help make this more subtle version of the objection clearer. Suppose that the national standards for civic education include students' ability to understand the origin and meaning of America's founding documents, the Declaration of Independence and the Constitution. From the perspective of today's citizens, many of whom presumably do not have a deep understanding of these documents, such standards seem desirable because they would apparently imply that the citizens of tomorrow would have a profound commitment to the political premises upon which the nation is based, a commitment that would enhance the solidarity of the body politic. But it is equally possible that such an understanding would foster skepticism among tomorrow's citizens about the values on which America was founded, once the motivations of the founders' beliefs and their full meaning came to be understood. In this case, the consequences of this policy are not experienced as good by future citizens. Even worse, those consequences would not even be experienced as good from the perspective of those whose democratic will formulated the policy in the first place.

This is the sort of unintended consequences that cannot be avoided by the alignment of capacity with will, for it assumes that such an alignment has taken place and that teachers have become capable of understanding these matters and teaching them to their students. Instead, it arises from the inevitable unpredictability of the effects of capacity on political will. In other words, changes in the capacity of teachers and other citizens can also create changes in their will, that is, in what they believe to be good. Thus, capacity is not simply an instrument for the achievement of a fixed and enduring political will. Indeed, this is the fundamental error on which democratic authoritarianism is based. Rather, capacity and will interact in significant and indeterminate ways. In addition, a justifiable account of democracy must recognize that capacity is as fundamental a concern of political theory as is political will.

Dewey proposed a different theory of democracy, one that I call democratic progressivism, that, it is argued in this chapter, is more justified in its approach to the aspirations and capacities of citizens than democratic authoritarianism. For Dewey, the hallmark of democracy lies in two related conditions of the society. A democracy is a social order that has the ability to recognize and to solve the public's problems as they emerge (Dewey, 1927). Such problems arise when the collective aspirations of the public, or its democratic will, is inconsistent with prevailing material and human conditions in a society, or its social capacity. In contract to democratic authoritarianism, however, Dewey does not understand these problems as a simple discrepancy between the antecedently defined democratic will and the social capacity to carry out that will at the particular time that the democratic will is articulated. Thus, solving a problem is not simply a matter of adjusting social capacity to the democratic will. Neither, of course, is problem solving simply a matter of making a virtue of necessity, that is, of adjusting the democratic will to the prevailing social capacity. Both of these versions of problem solving create a static rather than a progressive society, with the first assuming a static political will and the second a static social capacity. Instead, a progressive society is one in which democratic will and social capacity change continuously and in relation to one another. Thus, a truly democratic society not only reshapes human capacities to realize the collective aspirations of the public but it also permits those aspirations to evolve to take advantage of the possibilities implied by prevailing or emergent human capacities. For such a society to exist, democratic will and social capacity must be in creative tension with one another, and neither will nor capacity must be understood as fixed, permanent, or paramount in political importance.

The first condition of a progressive democratic society, therefore, is a degree of diversity in its citizens' beliefs about the good life for individuals and the society as a whole and in their theoretical and practical knowledge of the world. This diversity cannot be based on existing convention but instead on free and open inquiry. Without these kinds of diversity, there can be no creative tension between democratic will and social capacity and, thus, no possibility for the progressive evolution of either. That some citizens aspire for different goals from others opens up the possibility that the democratic will can change; when these differences are founded on inquiry, however imperfect and incomplete, argument and evidence can provide the means by which that change in the public will takes place. That the understandings and capabilities of some citizens are different from those of others opens up the possibility that social capacity can change, especially if such differences in capacity are the product of various kinds of intelligence developed through a process of publicly accessibly analysis and experimentation. Also, together these differences open up the further possibility that democratic will and social capacity can influence each other in mutual and progressive ways.

By itself, however, diversity founded on inquiry is not a sufficient condition for progressive democracy. If citizens with different aspirations and capabilities are isolated from one another, the mutual influence of democratic will and social capacity cannot be realized. Rather, sects of the like-minded and like-skilled will, at best, compete for political predominance; at worst, they will seek to end their political affiliation altogether. Thus, the second condition of progressive democracy is a high degree of interaction among a diverse citizenry (Dewey, 1916/1966). By means of open and robust interaction, alternative aspirations and the reasons that might justify them become generally available in the society. Likewise, such interaction permits the dissemination of capacities and their intellectual foundations. According to Dewey, democracy "will have its consummation when free social inquiry is indissolubly wedded to the art of full and moving communication" (1927, p. 184).

The theory of progressive democracy, thus, overcomes the shortcoming of democratic authoritarianism. It breaks the rigid and hierarchical relationship between political will and social capacity, while at the same time, preserving a legitimate and interactive connection between them. In particular, it provides a reasonable account of how democratic will can change, namely through the evolution of social capacity rather than merely through irrational changes in mass sentiment. In this way, it suggest that social policy should be assessed not merely for its ability to realize the prevailing political will in the short run, but also for its tendency to free the development of human intellectual and practical capabilities.[1]

Thus, progressive democracy casts suspicion on the extent to which the movement toward national standards in education focuses fundamentally on the creation of a coherent consensus about the goals and processes of the nation's schools. Such a focus represents an effort to make the public opinion of a particular time and place the keystone of education policy, an effort that ignores the way in which public sentiment evolves with social capacity and, most important, the salutary effect that an appropriately free development of social capacity can have on the aims and intention of the public. It also casts doubt on the national standards movement's treatment of the capacity of students, teachers, and other educators, and schools as a whole.

SCHOOLS AND SOCIAL CAPACITY

As already noted, the national standards movement, and the democratic authoritarianism in which it is rooted, conceive of social capacity solely as an instrument to the realization of democratic political will. Here, the capacities of citizens are nothing more than a way of creating the conditions specified by the current political consensus, and the capacity of schools to promote student learning is simply a means of producing the intended social capacity among tomorrow's citizens. The theory of progressive democracy, by contrast, recognizes the social capacity can change political will and that, under certain conditions (namely, those of open inquiry and free communication), such changes in political will are morally desirable. Here, the capacities of citizens are a source of new ideas about the purposes and possibilities of the society, and the capacity of schools to promote the learning of future citizens is itself a source of this evolving political will.

Thus, the development of social capacity in schools is not only a response to the democratic will but also a determinant of that will. To be sure, to assign schools, or any other agency, the responsibility for influencing political will is potentially risky, for the possibility of using this authority to enforce one's prejudices on others is both tempting and morally problematic. Dewey's proposed protections against this temptation are two. First schools have dual responsibility to yield to and to lead the political will. For this reason, an appropriate balance of responsiveness and leadership must inform the responsibilities of schools and teachers. For this reason, certain conceptions of teacher professionalism as autonomy from politics cannot be justified (Bull, 1990). Second, the source of schools' leadership of the development of student capacity is not the prejudices of individual teachers, administrators, or community members but the emerging social problems in individual communities and the society at large as experienced by students, their parents, and others in the local context. Open inquiry into these problems is to be the basis for the legitimate diversity that schools seek to foster, not simple conformity to the predetermined intentions of those who wish to use schools for their own narrow purposes. Seen in this light, then, a successful and progressive democracy depends on schools that enable students to respond in creative and responsible ways to the emerging problems of individuals and the society as a whole.

From this perspective, the national standards movement misconceives the schools' responsibilities toward their students' capacities. Schools' task is not just to develop in students a democratically defined configuration of knowledge and skill but also to open up the possibility of students' developing the new constellations of capacities needed to confront and resolve the society's emerging problems. But why not just incorporate *that* responsibility into the definition of the national standards? The answer to this question reveals why the national standards movement also misunderstands the capacities that teachers need in a progressive democracy.

As already noted, national standards for education as they are now conceived are not simply an articulation of general goals for schools and their students. In fact, the current impetus for national standards originated in part from dissatisfaction with the imprecision of the global goals adopted under the Bush administration's Education 2000 legislation. National standards represent an effort to provide a detailed specification of the outcomes, curriculum, and resources implied by such national goals. Thus, a goal of enabling students to develop capacities needed to confront and resolve emerging social problems is, at best, only the starting place for national standards. To become the basis for genuine standards of the type now under discussion, such a goal would need to be analyzed and delineated into the particular skills and knowledge that students need to acquire. But, of course, if we were able to accomplish such an analysis, we would already have to be able to solve the problems for which we need those particular capacities in tomorrow's citizens. The very premise of this goal, however, is that we do not now have the ability to solve these emerging problems. In other words, it is conceptually impossible to transform this goal into a set of national standards. For such standards are adequate to the solution of yesterday's and today's, but not tomorrow's, problems. This result should come as no real surprise; indeed, it is a logical consequence of Dewey's contention that democratic authoritarianism assumes a static society.

This result poses an apparent dilemma for schools and education policy makers. If the social capacity that we can specify in advance is inadequate to meet the demand of tomorrow and if schools in a progressive democracy are supposed to develop the capacity to meet those demands, schools seem to be faced with a task they cannot possibly achieve. But this task is impossible only on the assumption that schools can develop only those capacities that can be specified in advance.

For Dewey, these new capacities develop as students, teachers, schools, and other social organizations attempt to address what seem to be society's emerging problems where and when they appear. In at least part of the educational enterprise, then, students and teachers need to think about and work on those problems. But the problems of tomorrow cannot be specified any more accurately than the capacities needed to resolve them can. Thus, it is critical to a progressive democracy that multiple and diverse efforts to anticipate and conceptualize those problems be encouraged.

On the one hand, here lies the importance to progressive democracy of local control and diversity, for local teachers, schools, and communities are the well-spring of these multiple efforts to define and address new problems. On this account, local autonomy is not simply an expression of a right of self-governance. Beyond this, such autonomy makes a potential contribution to the nation as a whole through localities' efforts to anticipate, communicate, and resolve problems that may turn out to be pervasive. On the other hand, the necessity for localities to engage in such efforts has implications for the capacities of teachers that extend far beyond the accounts provided by the national standards movement.

We have seen that teacher capacity has a specific meaning and value from the perspective of national standards—namely, the particular configuration of subject matter knowledge and pedagogical skill necessary to enable students to meet the standards. But if teachers are to play a key role in local efforts to anticipate the problems of tomorrow, such a view of teacher capacity is seriously incomplete. Just as students' capacities to engage in this task cannot be specified in advance, neither can those of teachers. Moreover, the role of teachers cannot be limited to the promulgation of specified knowledge and skills. They, too, must be expected to think about and work on their communities' emerging problems. The lessons here are that in a progressive democracy, teachers' capacities should not be conceived as a predefined set of skills and their professional roles should not be construed as the simple accomplishment of predetermined result by predetermined means. Yet, as we have noted, that is precisely how the national standards movement tends to regard these matters.

In contrast, progressive democracy sees teachers' capacities as needing to evolve in indeterminate and locally responsive ways. This local response must be more than simply an attempt to adapt their teaching techniques and their students' abilities to a set of outcomes specified by the current state of the national political will. Rather, this response must include an effort to understand the emerging problems of their schools and communities, to address those problems in their teaching, and to communicate their findings to a wider audience of teachers and citizens as hypotheses about the society's emerging problems and their solutions. In this way, teachers and schools make a legitimate contribution to the political will; they do not simply serve that will.

Indeed, some current ideas about the professional development of teachers represent teacher capacity and the teacher's professional role in precisely these ways.[2] With adequate district leadership and support, teachers, in this view, are to develop their capacities to diagnose the problems and possibilities of their own schools and to respond creativity and intelligently to them. Of course, these tasks cannot be accomplished by individual teachers working alone but rather by teachers working in concert with community members and their teaching colleagues. In an important sense, the standards movement's view of teacher capacity constrains teacher development into narrow channels defined by the standards. This alternative view, by contrast, unleashes the intellectual and practical talents of teachers to work on the problems of their schools and communities, to develop their students' capacities in ways that are relevant to those problems, and, thereby, to contribute to the progressive change of both political will and social capacity.

SCHOOLS AND EQUAL OPPORTUNITY

The national standards movement also holds that shaping social capacity in line with the prevailing political will can enhance the achievement of equal educational opportunity.[3] The current incoherent state of school expectations for students, curricular opportunities available to them, and school resources, ensure that many socially and economically disadvantaged children will only have their disadvantages magnified in schools. Uniform expectations for students and schools coupled with the provision of resources sufficient to the realization of those expectations should, it is asserted, overcome students' unfair disadvantages in attaining socially important qualifications and eventually, the positions in society to which they are relevant.

Of course, progressive democrats would be similarly concerned about the unfair conditions that many students currently face in schools. But they would have grave doubts about the sufficiency of the standards movement's proposed remedies. First, they would be skeptical that the achievement of national standards would truly equalize social opportunity. In the very short run, equal opportunity may involve chances to achieve intellectual and practical attainments already known to be socially advantageous. In the long run, however, such attainments are not likely to sustain their social advantage because the capacities that carry such advantage are constantly changing as social values and social capacity evolve. Thus, what the disadvantaged need is not just a chance to acquire the abilities that society values and rewards today but, more important, the abilities relevant to tomorrow.[4] Furthermore, uniform national standards may actually prevent their developing these capacities of future advantage. After all, advantaged students already have a head start toward the achievement of national standards; therefore, their schools will have the luxury of dealing extensively with skills and knowledge not covered by the standards, or in other words, with the possible capacities of future advantage. As schools and classrooms for the disadvantaged focus intensively and narrowly on the attainment of national standards, however, as they must in order to meet them, the disadvantaged will be systematically deprived of opportunities to develop these capacities of future advantage. In other words, even if schools succeed in helping the disadvantaged attain the national standards in the short run, these students will remain disadvantaged in the long run.

Second, progressive democrats would be suspicious that the very conception of equal opportunity embraced by the national standards movement is itself responsible for the maintenance of unequal opportunity in the society. Essentially, the national standards movement suggests that there is a single ladder of social opportunity to be climbed—namely, the ladder defined by the national standards. A single, authoritative ladder of opportunity makes it almost inevitable that citizens' opportunities will remain unequal, partly because it is a natural fact that people do differ in their capacities but, more importantly, because existing social and economic advantage can be brought to bear more effectively when the competition for social advantage is so narrowly defined.

Progressive democrats conceive of social opportunity as involving multiple pathways to success, some of which have not yet emerged. They view the equalization of opportunity not as trying to give all children the same advantages in climbing a single ladder of success but as trying to ensure that no single pathway gains exclusive social and political authority over all others. The maintenance of public schools in which teachers, community members, and students are working seriously to define the problems and possibilities of the future as they appear in local communities and to develop new configurations of capacity to meet them is one important way in which progressive democracies can maintain multiple and alternative pathways to success. It is important to note that these schools do not merely maintain local differences for their own sake. Rather, the different capacities developed in schools of a progressive democracy are genuine, if not guaranteed, pathways to success because they are developed as reasonable responses to emerging social conditions. Thus, the approach to the development of social capacity taken by progressive democracies stands at least a reasonable chance of equalizing opportunity understood in this way; the approach to capacity development taken by the national standards movement seems doomed to failure even by its own definition of equal opportunity.

CONCLUSION

No one is in favor of low standards, least of all progressive democrats. In addition no one is in favor of teachers who do not apply their full talents to the development of their students' capacities. The view of student and teacher capacity taken by the proponents of national standards, however, is short sighted. In assuming that the best way to realize high standards is to impose a uniform definition of student achievement and school curriculum on the nation's schools, this movement willy-nilly embraces a version of democracy that prioritizes political will over social capacity and that, therefore, prizes social inertia and makes inequalities of opportunity a permanent and insoluble problem.

By contrast, the theory of progressive democracy sees schools, teachers, and students as resources in the concomitant evolution of social capacity and political will. When schools take local issues seriously and seek to develop new configurations of teacher and student capacity to understand and resolve those issues, schools not only respond to their localities but also contribute to the national dialogue about what is valuable and feasible for the society as a whole. In effect, localities whose schools act in this way engage in a practical effort to tentatively define what standards ought to be.

National subject matter organizations and national teacher groups can also make important contributions to the debate over standards. But it is a mistake for the federal government to attempt to congeal the national democratic will around any one such hypothesis about the standards that are most appropriate for the nation. Instead, federal policy might more profitably focus attention and resources on the open-ended development of student and teacher capacity.

NOTES

1. This advantage of progressive democracy does not necessarily mean that it is without faults. For example, it may assume that social change under these conditions is necessarily progressive in some metaphysically teleological sense. It also seems to lack a suitable account of citizens' liberties. For an account of democracy that captures some of Dewey's insights but that avoids teleology and embraces certain traditional liberal values, see A. Gutmann and D. Thompson, *Democracy and Disagreement* (Cambridge, MA: Belknap Press, 1996).

2. See B. Bull and M. Buechler, *Learning Together*: Professional Development for Better Schools (Bloomington: Indiana Education Policy Center, 1996) for a summary of this line of research and argument.

3. This assertion is explicit in Smith and O'Day, 1991.

4. See Barry Bull, "Is systemic reform in education morally justifiable?" *Studies in Philosophy and Education 15* (1996), 13–23 for a similar argument.

REFERENCES

Berman, P., & McLaughlin, M. (1975–78). *Federal programs supporting educational change,* volumes I–VIII. Santa Monica: The Rand Corporation.

Bull, B. (1990). The limits of teacher professionalization, In J. Goodlad, R. Soder, & K. Sirotnik (Eds.), *The moral dimensions of teaching* (pp. 87–129). San Francisco: Jossey Bass.

Clune, W. H. (1993). The best path to systemic educational policy: Standardized/centralized or differentiated/decentralized. *Educational Evaluation and Policy Analysis*, 15, 233–254.

Dahl, R. (1971). *Polyarchy: Participation and opposition* New Haven: Yale University Press.

Dewey, J. (1927). *The public and its problems.* Denver, CO: Alan Swallow.

Dewey, J. (1966). *Democracy and education.* New York: Free Press. (Original work published 1916)

Fuhrman, S., Clune, W., & Elmore, R. (1988). Research on education reform: Lessons on the implementation of policy. In D. Monk and J. Underwood (Eds.), *Micro-level school finance: Issues and implications for policy* Cambridge: MA: Ballinger.

Goals 2000: Educate America Act (1994). [Online]. Available: www.ed.gov/legislation/GOALS 2000/The Act.

Hegel, G. W. F. (1942). *The philosophy of right* (T.M. Knox, Trans.), Oxford: Claredon Press. (Original work published 1821)

Kant, I. (1964). *Groundwork of the metaphysic of morals* (H. J. Paton Trans.) New York: Harper. (Original work published 1785)

Marx, K., & Engels, F. (1972). *The communist manifesto* In R. C. Tucker (Ed.) *The Marx Engels reader* (pp. 331–362). New York: Norton. (Original work published 1848)

National Commission for Excellence in Education. (1983). *A nation at risk: The imperatives for educational reform.* Washington, DC: United States Government Printing Office.

Rousseau, J. J. (1950). *The social contract and discourses* (1–142) (G. D. H. Cole, Trans.) New York: Dutton. (Original work published 1762)

Smith, M. S., & O'Day, J. (1991). Systemic school reform. In S. Fuhrman & B. Malen (Eds.), *The Politics of Curriculum and Testing* (pp. 233–267) London: Taylor & Francis.

8

SCHOOL CHANGE BUSINESS AND THE PRIVATE PUSH

Bruce Anthony Jones
University of Missouri–Columbia

Susan Otterbourg
Delman Communication

In the early 1980s, the business community embarked on an unprecedented level of involvement in the education affairs of the nation's schools. The primary goals of business involvement in education has always been to aid in the improvement of school performance and student achievement. There is, however, no systematic evaluation of whether or not business has achieved these goals. Despite this, there remain assertions throughout the literature from numerous scholars, practitioners, and policy makers on the *vital importance of business in education.* The purpose of this chapter is to provide a conceptual context for understanding the role of business in education and to suggest critical policy issues and challenges associated with the assessment of this role.

Overall, there are two levels of business involvement in education that warrant examination. At onc level, businesses have operated to influence education from a national platform. At another level, business involvement has occurred at a local community level. Key evaluative questions to ask include: (1) What is the impact of the business community that operates at a national level on the relationships and activities between business and public education at the local level? (2) What are the common trends and types of business involvement in public education at the national and local community levels? (3) How have the programmatic activities associated with these trends and types of business involvement influenced school achievement (i.e., business impact on school management practices, school climate, curriculum, and student achievement)? (4) What methodological and thematic issues exist for efforts to engage in comprehensive evaluations of education-business partnerships?

To address these questions, the first section of this chapter discusses the recent context and influence of business involvement in public education at the national level. This includes a discussion of the business–education agenda and major organizational vehicles used to advance this agenda on a national scale. In the second section, business involvement in public education at the local level is discussed. Data for this section is drawn from two national assessments of education-partnership initiatives. These education-partnership initiatives were broad in scope and not limited to school–business partnership efforts. Therefore, the focus on the assessment of these initiatives is only on those education-partnerships that included some level of business involvement.

The third section of this chapter discusses the business-education agenda at the national level and compares it to school–business activity at the local and community level. In this regard, emphasis is on the extent to which is there a match or mismatch between business involvement in education at the national level and at local levels. In light of this, issues for evaluation are discussed in the final section.

IN THE BEGINNING: EVOLUTION OF INVOLVEMENT

Business has always been a major stakeholder relative to the products of America's public education system, taking it for granted that schools as well as post-secondary education and training institutions would supply a workforce that fulfilled its requirements [Committee for Economic Development (CED), 1985; Gelberg, 1997].

Prior to the 1980s, business involvement in education at both the national and local levels was largely unfocused, project-based, episodic, special purpose, tacked on, and usually, at the periphery of schools' core technology of teaching and learning. A high estimate of corporate support to schools was half of 1 percent of its giving programs; large city corporate involvement reported a mean of $800,000 (Press, 1983, p. 3).

Traditionally, some businesses were represented on boards of education; were involved in parent/teacher association activities; supported the passage of school budgets and bond issues, the replacement of playground and band equipment, and beautification projects; purchased or donated materials; and aided and honored teachers (Halperin & Merenda, 1986; Jones, 1994).

Another indication of the relatively low level of business support of public education was revealed in a 1982 survey conducted by the School Management Group. Business was the least likely community cluster to volunteer in public schools.

1. School volunteers were found in 79 percent of the nation's public school districts.
2. Approximate percentages of different groups of people who volunteered in schools averaged as follows: parents (39%); older citizen taxpayers (24%); students (21%); and business employees (18%) (Halperin & Merenda, 1986).

Changing Times

But times have changed. The business push for massive education reform has been fueled in part by economic and political changes in the global economy. The work place is being transformed as the economy shifts from a manufacturing economy to a technology and service-based economy. This shift, plus stiff global competition, major corporate structural reengineering, reduced discretionary government resources, and increasingly complex workforce requirements, place new demands on corporate America and how it views the workplace. At a national level, business views the formation of partnerships with schools as one of many ways in which these changes can be addressed. Schools are viewed as the best institutions to prepare students to meet the challenges associated with these workforce changes.

According to the National Alliance of Business (1991), underqualified, poorly trained workers diminish productivity and increase remediation and supervision costs. Each year's class of dropouts already costs the nation over $260 billion in lost earnings and foregone taxes. Moreover, relative to the past, there are fewer lower-skilled jobs for individuals who lack an advanced education. This is especially the case in industry and service fields, which now require higher-level skills. Eighty-six percent of these current jobs that require professional, technological, or managerial skills are expanding, while 93 percent of blue collar jobs are contracting ("Business response," 1989; Reich, 1992).

The nation is experiencing a tighter labor market that seeks higher wages and incentives to increase its productivity. A predicted shortage of over 23 million young Americans able and willing to fill the jobs that will exist by the year 2000 is a serious cause for concern. Higher proportions of entering workforce in the United States appear to lack the skills, behaviors, and attitudes that will enable them to perform the jobs required. This *growing educational underclass* [Committee on Economic Development (CED), 1987, p. ix] that cannot meet even minimal workforce qualifications, restricts business' ability to compete and to grow (CED, 1985; Hart, 1994; Johnson & Linden, 1992).

Clearly, business is directly dependent on the knowledge and expertise of its workforce to maintain the technological edge that enables the United States to compete successfully in a global economy. The downsizing of over 90 percent of companies since the early 1990s may reduce the demand for large numbers of new workers, but not the need for the qualified workers that these companies hire. According to corporate executive, Lee Iacocca, "In a high-tech world we compete in, the biggest edge is not cheap labor, but well-educated labor" (Alster & Brothers, 1992, p. 7).

NATIONAL THRUSTS: SINCE THE 1980s

The decade of the 1980s represents the single most significant decade in United States history whereby business pushed for the need to advance massive education reform. The flurry of business involvement in education also came in the immediate aftermath of the *Nation at Risk* report. The United States Department of Education released this report in 1983. The report essentially proclaimed that the nation's schools were in a state of crisis (Levine, 1985). According to Orlich (1989, p. 513, 516) "by the mid 1980s more than 275 education task forces had been formed . . . at least 18 books or book-length reports intended to *fix the schools* were published . . . approximately 700 pieces of legislation were enacted between 1983 and 1985 alone—all to reform the schools and those who work in them."

In the context of the environment described, the Reagan administration strongly urged more involvement of business in education as a partial strategy to substitute federal support of education with business support. This urging culminated at the start of the 1983 to 1984 school year when he declared that school year the *year of partnerships in education*. In 1984, 42,000 partnerships were recorded in elementary and secondary schools; by 1988, over 140,800 were reported by the United States Department of Education. Fifty-seven percent of these programs were sponsored by business organizations. By school years 1987 to 1990, over half (51%) of the nation's school districts with approximately 29.7 million students had active partnership programs (McNett, 1982; NAPE, 1991; Reingold, 1990).

Increasingly, businesses see the need for good schools as a "bottom-line" issue. Partnerships in education, previously primarily a function of community relations and corporate philanthropy, are emerging as the province of human resources. Accordingly, business sees itself as an "investor" rather than a "contributor" to education (Berebeim, 1991, p. 10; see also Doyle, 1994; Lund, 1988).

Business has also begun to refocus its involvement in education on "outcomes" (demonstrated results) rather than "inputs" (how many students or educators are served, programs stated dollars spent). Business is beginning to understand the need for the following.

1. Long-term comprehensive changes in the management and delivery of instruction in the classroom and in school governance.
2. Replication and leveraging of good practices to bring small initiatives "to scale."
3. Institutionalization of exemplary efforts beyond the grant period or the vision and leadership of the effort's founder (Edelstein, 1989; Lund, 1988; NAB, 1991; Nugent & Rigden, 1994; USDOL, 1995).

At a national level, four umbrella business organizations have played a key role in advancing these trends since the early 1980s. These organizations are the Committee on Economic Development (CED), the Conference Board, the Business Roundtable, and the National Alliance of Business (NAB). Each of these organizations worked to have an impact on education reform as it relates to their own collective and distinctive missions. For example, in varying degrees, through these umbrella organizations, the business community advanced calls for the need for schools across the nation to adopt nationally crafted education standards.

Committee on Economic Development

With the Committee on Economic Development (CED) publication *Investing in our children: Business and the public schools*, the business community for the first time became integrally involved with developing detailed methods for the improvement of the nation's schools (Ray & Mickelson, 1989). This was the first time CED had anything to say about education in over 15 years (Timpane, 1984). In the aftermath of the CED report, according to the Business Roundtable (1990), over 300 reports were commissioned by various segments of the business community on *what schools need to do to improve*.

The Conference Board

The Conference Board is a membership organization comprised of the largest businesses in the United States as its members. The Conference Board serves in a research and convening role around issues in education for its business members and select individuals from the education community. Each year, the Conference Board convenes a *business–education* conference on K–12 public education. The conference, along with the host of publications on education that are disseminated by the Conference Board, aid in defining the kinds of issues and priorities that business needs to establish within the education arena. In 1991, The Conference Board created its annual *Best in Class Awards*, which are designed to recognize companies that show commitment and leadership (through the giving of resources, time, and talent) in business–education partnerships that address the improvement of primary and secondary education as follows.

- Investing in innovative programs that advance education improvement through school reform.
- Providing leadership at state and local levels to strengthen business–education goals.
- Contributing leadership in preschool and early childhood education.
- Supporting improved teaching of science, mathematics, and technology in the public schools.
- Mobilizing nationwide support for education improvement.

The Business Roundtable

The Business Roundtable exerted heavy influence on the policy agenda of the First Education Summit of Governors convened by President Bush in 1989. The Business Roundtable is comprised of the chief executive officers of 200 of the largest corporations in the United States. The Business Roundtable agenda was three-fold: (1) advance national education policy standards; (2) provide resources to advance these national standards across the nation; and (3) work with state governors to ensure that these standards were executed (The Business Roundtable, 1990). In 1990, the Business Roundtable established nine components for schools systems to enact in what was to become known as the *Essential Components of a Successful School System*. These components are as follows.

1. Schools are to be committed to four operating assumptions, all students can learn at significantly higher levels, we know how to teach all students successfully, curriculum content must reflect high expectations for all students, and every child must have an advocate.
2. The new system is performance- or outcome-based with an emphasis on standards.
3. Assessment strategies must be as strong and rich as the outcomes (*assessment*).
4. Schools should receive rewards for success, assistance to improve, and consequences for failure (*accountability*).
5. School-based staff members have a major role in making instructional decisions (*school-based decision making*).
6. Major emphasis is placed on staff development.
7. A high quality prekindergarten program is established, at least for all disadvantaged students.
8. Health and other social services are sufficient to reduce significant barriers to learning.
9. Technology is used to raise student and teacher productivity and to expand access to learning technology.

States were to be held to these national standards through a *gap analysis* approach to accountability. The gap analysis was to serve as a benchmark for determining the *gap* between where states were in relation to how far they needed to go in order to achieve the nine *essential components of a successful school system* listed previously. Thirty-eight states adopted statewide reform on the basis of these nine components (Gelberg, 1997).

Keeping in line with calls from the business community to implement national standards for education, in 1994, President Clinton (who chaired the first Presidential Education Summit as Governor of Arkansas) signed one of the most massive pieces of education legislation in history. Public Law 103-227, entitled *Goals 2000: Educate America Act,* included the establishment of a National Education Standards and Improvement Council to establish and monitor efforts of state systems to execute national standards.

The National Alliance of Business

The National Alliance of Business (NAB) engages in public advocacy on business–education issues with a primary emphasis on school-to-work concerns. Essential to the school-to-work agenda is the question of whether or not children are academically and socially prepared to enter the workforce. In 1995, the National Alliance of Business released a report entitled, *The Challenge of Change: Standards to Make Education Work for All Our Children*. In similar fashion to the Business Roundtable report, this report contained nine principles for school reform. The report emphasized a common set of national standards for all schools.

1. All students should be given the opportunity to master challenging academic subject matter calibrated against world-class education standards.
2. There must be one set of standards for all students.
3. Standards must have a common core of skills.
4. Standards must reflect *real world* requirements.
5. Standards must be voluntary.
6. Standards must be dynamic.
7. Standards must include criteria against which performance is measured.
8. Business leaders must have a seat at the table.
9. Standards and performance measures must be understood and supported by parents and the general public (National Alliance of Business, 1995).

LOCAL THRUSTS: SINCE THE 1980s

Two national assessments of "local" education–community partnerships have been conducted over the past 10 years. One assessment utilized a survey approach to determine how many and what types of education partnerships developed between 1983 to 1984 and 1987 to 1988. The second assessment draws data from the largest funded education-partnership initiative in United States history. Both assessments were developed and funded by the United States Department of Education.

Neither assessment focuses specifically on school–business involvement because the two initiatives involved numerous school–community partnership configurations (i.e., school–media, school–university, school–parent, school–community-based organizations, etc.). This section draws data from components of both assessments that list business involvement.

National Center for Education Statistics (NCES) Survey

In 1988, the National Center for Education Statistics (NCES) conducted a national assessment through survey method of education–community partnerships. A stratified sample of 1,574 regular public elementary and secondary schools were mailed surveys that requested information on the types of partnering institutions and partnership activities in place at the school. Survey respondents were requested to provide this data for the years 1983 to 1984 and 1987 to 1988.

NCES Data Results

The NCES survey data revealed that business at the local level played an active partnership role. Fifty-four percent of the partnerships reported by the school principal respondents were with the business sector.[1] The two most frequent types of business support of education provided by business were guest speakers, special demonstrations, or use of partners' facilities or equipment (including tours); and special awards, scholarships, or incentives for students (Table 8.1). Areas where business was less involved included professional development of teachers, work-studies or summer employment initiatives for students, academic tutoring of students, and provision of computers and other material resources for schools.

Educational Partnership Program

With the United States Congression passage of the Education Partnership Act (1988), the United States Department of Education launched the Educational

TABLE 8.1.
Percentage of Education Partnerships Providing Various Types of Support by Characteristic Nces Survey to School Districts (1987–1988)

School Program Characteristic

	Awards/ scholarships, incentives, for students	Work studies of summer employment for students	Academic tutoring of students	Assistance for students with special needs	Guest speakers demonstrations, use of partners facilities/tours	Computers, other equipment, or books
Total	44	11	12	17	45	14
	Contribute employees as teachers	Sponsor special awards for teachers or schools	Grants for teachers	Contribute to professional development of school staff	Serve on education committee/task force	Other
Total	10	12	5	9	16	4

Source: NCES, 1989.

Partnership Program (EPP). The EPP is the largest public education community partnership initiative in Unites States history. The assessment of this initiative "represents the largest and most extended evaluation of educational partnerships that exists" (Southwest Regional Laboratory, 1995, p. 2). A total of 29 public school localities across the United States were provided *partnership* grants between 1990 to 1993 to plan and implement community partnership activities in support of school reform. Twenty-one of the 29 partnership initiatives included the local business sector as a key player in partnership program goals and objectives.

EPP Data Results

Overall, the 29 EPP sites attempted to advance two broad goals: (1) to prepare students for "adult responsibility"; and (2) to enhance teacher professionalism by providing opportunities for teachers to share knowledge with each other and others in the community. To achieve these two goals, program activities were developed between school authorities and members of the local communities under the following program category areas: alternative education, curriculum reform, teacher and or administrator professional development, speakers bureau, and systemic reform.

Table 8.2 reveals that business involvement with effort to engage in school reform focused largely in the category of curriculum reform and teacher and administrator professional development. In curriculum reform, the overwhelming emphasis was on school-to-work programming for students and a focus on improving technology literacy. At some sites, curriculum reform included a substantial involvement of professional volunteers, tutors, or mentors from the community. In the area of

TABLE 8.2.

Reported Number of Education Partnerships Foci by Category with Some Level of Business Involvement The Educational Partnerships Program (1990–1993)

Category						
Alternative Education	Curriculum		Professional Development		Speakers Bureau	Systemic Reform
1	• School-to-work	9	• Administration	2	1	3
	• Science, math, and technology	6	• Classroom practice	2		
	• Volunteers, tutors, and mentors	3	• Technology	2		
Total 1		**18**		**6**	**1**	**3**

Source: Educational Partnerships Program, 1994.

professional development, business worked with efforts to improve overall school governance (in one instance business provided training in total quality management (TQM), teacher classroom practice, and also, technology literacy.

The EPP evaluation did not reveal whether or not the program results described previously improved the overall performance of the schools. The evaluation also did not reveal how the program influenced student achievement. The emphasis of the evaluation was on the success of the partnering effort, that is, how well the partners collaborated with each other as opposed to how well schools performed and student achievement improved. In this respect, "partnering efforts" and the degree to which success was met in effort to collaborate around school reform was most affected by:

1. The extent that there was early commitment to a shared vision of partnership goals (massive systemic change versus limited program implementation) and which target groups (students, teachers, schools, and community) would become program beneficiaries of these goals.
2. The extent that there was general agreement on who and what resources would serve as catalyst(s) for reform [usage of internal (local) expertise or external expertise].
3. The extent to which there was continuity among key partnership members. Member turnover more often than not had a negative effect on the partnering effort.
4. The resource stability of the school districts (human, fiscal, and material resources available.
5. The general economic stability of the community.
6. The stability of the local economy with specific regard to the stability of those businesses that participated as partners.

BUSINESS AT THE NATIONAL LEVEL AND BUSINESS AT THE LOCAL LEVEL

Throughout the decade of the 1980s, key business organizations at a national level called for the need for curriculum reform with an emphasis on science, mathematics, technology, and computer literacy; adoption of national standards for school achievement with measurable outcomes; more professional development of teachers and administrators; and accountability of school officials (teachers and administrators) relative to demands to meet this reform and student achievement. The school, community, and family initiatives implemented by International Business Machine (IBM), Phillips Petroleum Corporation, and of WFD, Inc. serve as examples of how business is working to advance student achievement and school reform.

International Business Machine (IBM) launched the *Reinventing Education 1 Initiative* in 1994 and *Reinventing Education 2 Initiative* in 1997. Under the auspices of these initiatives, a total of 22 school districts from across the nation are the recipients of over $10 million in school reform grants. The primary goal of the Reinventing Education Initiative is to use new applications of technology to develop and institutionalize school reform in a way that improves student achievement. These technology applications are used to deal with school and parental involvement in education issues and to provide better instructional tools for teachers in math, science, and reading.

The more recent push toward accountability is exemplified by Phillips Petroleum Corporation. Phillips Petroleum is headquartered in the United States and operates in the United States and 37 countries overseas. Two themes have emerged with its strategic planning on corporate giving. One theme is "focus." The other theme is "accountability." In the distant past, the corporation distributed scholarship grants for high school students to attend the University of Oklahoma. Minimal accountability requirements were attached to the scholarships. Often, student recipients were unaware of the source of the scholarships. More recently, the scholarship program has been given a name, "Phillips Scholars Program" and a focus. The focus is on minority students who are under-represented in the areas of mathematics, accounting, geology, and geophysics. The students may be selected from any location in the United States. To meet the accountability requirements, the corporation provides employee mentors to the student beneficiaries of the Phillips Scholars Program.

The growth of business involvement in education reform is revealed in the work by WFD, Inc. WFD, Inc. works substantially in the area of parental development concerns and how these concerns link to student achievement. Through its Life-Works initiative, over 26,000 corporate employees are provided consultation and referral services related to family development issues. Since 1990, the WFD, Inc. has managed the investment of approximately $24 million in corporate dollars to help meet the needs of working parents with school-aged children. According to a WFD, Inc. representative, "companies want to ensure that they can find future employees who are competent in most areas and skilled in specific areas. Therefore, companies have been significant forces in the effort to develop state and national education standards."

Although local business involvement with public education as revealed with the data provided in Tables 8.1 and 8.2 are different assessment data sets and assessment methods, they do show a significant trend relative to the calls for reform by business at the national level. There has been an evolution of emphasis by business at the local level on school reform from one data set to the next. In the earlier years (1983 to 1984 and 1987 to 1988), Table 8.1 shows business involvement at the local level with a primary emphasis on providing "awards/scholarships and incentives for students to achieve academically" and "guest speakers with (education) tours of (business) facilities" (National Center for Education Statistics, 1989, pp. 18–43). In later years (1990 to 1993), according to Table 8.2, business involvement occurs with a primary emphasis on curriculum reform and professional development.

The calls by business at a national level to get *more substantially involved in education reform* may have helped to influence the shift just described. The earlier NCES survey data shows an emphasis by local business with school districts on "symbolic-feel-good" type activities (awards programs, business demonstrations, and guest speakers). By the time of the EPP initiative, business at the local level appeared more willing to get involved more substantially in education reform, including areas such as curriculum reform; professional development for teachers and administrators; improvement of technology literacy for teachers, students, and administrators, and volunteer and mentoring activities. The earlier NCES survey data showed minimal business involvement at the local level in these latter program areas.

In the area of "adoption of national standards" and "accountability" there may be less of a match at a local level with calls at a national level. The reasons for a lack of a match with the latter two areas are certainly reflected in political trends with regard to the recent and growing public perception and resentment toward the federal government intruding in the lives of individual citizens.

By the time of the second presidential education summit in March, 1996, a public backlash emerged against anything that was nationally motivated and perceived to be nationally controlled. Although the national business umbrella organizations supported and advanced the national standards movement, the idea of *national standards* was fast becoming a theme of the past. This backlash occurred with the rising influence of groups associated with the politically conservative right. These groups historically mistrusted big government and emphasized *local government control* of all matters that pertained to the lives of individual citizens (this includes a primary emphasis on demands for local control of education) (Immerwahr, 1994; Portner, 1995).

In this environment, the business community began to retreat from calls for national standards. For example, by the time of the second education summit, the Business Roundtable retreated from its 10-year commitment to ensuring the execution at the state level of the nationally established nine *Essential Goals for a Successful School*. The emphasis of discussion at the second education summit was on the need for *states to do their own thing* relative to high academic standards, technology and computer literacy in education reform. Education leaders who operated at a national level, such as the United States Secretary of Education, were uncharacteristically silent at the second summit. In the wake of all of this, the United States Congress defunded and dismantled the National Education Goals Panel (Harp, 1996).

Later in the year (September, 1996), the Business Roundtable, the National Alliance of Business (NAB), and the United States Chamber of Commerce issued a joint policy statement entitled, *A Common Agenda for Improving American*

Education. The tone of the statement was in line with the tone of the second presidential education summit. There is no mention of a call for national standards. The report emphasizes the need for business to facilitate education reform that is *locally driven*. The three organizations committed themselves to: (1) helping educators and policy makers set tough academic standards; (2) assessing student and school-system performance against these standards; and (3) using information to improve schools and create accountability, including rewards for success and consequences for failure (The Business Roundtable, 1996).

Issues for Policy and Assessment

This contribution points to the need for a more rigorous assessment of education–business partnerships. The effort to assess education–business partnerships here was problematic for two reasons. First, although business involvement was substantial, the information used here to assess business involvement at the local level was drawn from assessments that did not focus specifically on business involvement; evaluations need to be implemented that focus specifically on business and the schools. Second, data sets used with this contribution from the two different periods of time seem to show a changing emphasis of business involvement at the local level on school reform. We cannot be sure, however, because the data from each period stem from different samples and were collected using different assessment techniques. Moreover, with both assessments there was too much of an emphasis on *types* of community involvement with education and the partnering *process* as opposed to the actual *impact* of these partnerships on school performance and student achievement. Given this, evaluations of education–business partnerships need to be designed so that they directly address the impact of partnering on student and school achievement.

The business community is not monolithic. The assesment of education–business partnerships will need to take into account the policy impact of the business community at a national level and the impact of the business community at a local level on education. For example, what is the *partnering* relationship and impact of the business community at a national level on federal and state education policy? What are the motivations? How does this influence the education–business partnership agenda at the local level?

Assessment work is needed in the area of analyzing education–business partnerships in the context of the national and local business economy. Berlinder and Biddle (1996) address the need to develop such analysis, particularly in urban areas where business is downsized and schools continue to fail. According to Rich (1996), there is a great need to recognize that schools do not operate in a vacuum.

[often] the dreadful financial condition of public schools follows economic decline. . . . In order to create good schools, a stable economy is necessary. Without a stable

economy, it is difficult to maintain good schools. Inadequate schools create weak entry-level labor market candidates. A city with poorly trained workers finds it nearly impossible to attract new investors (a vicious circle). (p. 136)

Moreover, significant downturns in the local economies had a devastating effect on at least four of the 29 Educational Partnership Programs (EPP).

Finally, from a conceptual and practical standpoint, evaluation is needed in order to match the need to know the impact of business on education reform in relation to the rhetoric that speaks to how vital education–business partnerships are. Scholars, practitioners, and policy makers continue to write and speak about the importance of business involvement in education relative to student achievement and school performance. There remains little evaluative data to fully support these writings and contentions.

NOTES

1. This heavy involvement by business supports the results of another report on education-business partnerships. According to Kuhn (1990) a survey of Fortune 500 companies revealed that all but 7 of the 305 respondents reported partnership activity with school districts.

REFERENCES

Alster, J., & Brothers, T. (Eds.). (1992). *Saluting corporate achievements in education leadership.* New York: The Conference Board.

Berebeim, R. E. (1991). *Corporate strategies for improving public education.* (Rep. No. 970). New York: The Conference Board.

Berlinder, D. C., & Biddle, B. J. (1997). *The manufactured crisis: Myths, fraud, and the attack on America's public schools.* New York: Longman Publishers.

Business response to education in America. (1989). *Fortune 120,* 121–131.

The Business Roundtable. (1990). *Improving education in America.* Washington, DC: The Business Roundtable.

The Business Roundtable. (1996). *A common agenda for improving American education.* Washington, DC: The Business Roundtable.

Committee on Economic Development (CED). (1985). *Investing in our children: Business and the public schools.* New York: Author.

Doyle, D. (1994, Autumn). Developing human capital: The role of the private sector. *Theory into Practice, 33,* 218–226.

Edelstein, F. S. (1989). *A blueprint for business on restructuring education.* Washington, DC: National Alliance of Business.

Gelberg, D. (1979). The "business" of reforming American schools. New York: SUNY Press.

Halperin, S., & Merenda, D. (1986, Fall). Noble allies: Volunteers in the schools. *Basic Education: Issues, Answers and Facts, 2,* 1–6.

Harp, L. (1996, February). Summit seeks new focus on school reform. *Education Week, XV,* 1, 17.

Hart, M. (Ed.). (1994). *Partnerships for a prepared workforce: A conference report.* (Rep. No. 1078-94-CH). New York: The Conference Board.

Johnson, A. A., & Linden, F. (1992). *Availability of a quality workforce.* (Rep. No.1010). New York: The Conference Board.

Jones, B. A. (1994). The multiple constituency concept of collaboration: Influences of race, class, gender, and ethnicity. *Theory into Practice, 33,* 227–234.

Immerwahr, J. (1994). *The broken contract: Connecticut citizens look at public education.* New York: Public Agenda Foundation.

Kuhn, S. E. (1990). How business helps schools. *Fortune, 121,* 91–94.

Levine, M. (1985). A conceptual framework. In M. Levine (Ed.), *The private sector in public school: Can it improve education* (pp. 7–19). Washington, DC: American Enterprise Institute for Public Policy Research.

Lund, L. (1988). *Beyond business/education partnerships: The business experience.* (Rep. No. 918). New York: The Conference Board.

McNett, I. E. (1982). *Let's not reinvent the wheel: Profiles of school/business collaboration.* Washington, DC: Institute for Educational Leadership.

National Alliance of Business. (1995). *The challenge of change: Standards to make education work for all our children.* Washington, DC: Author.

National Alliance of Business. (1991). *The Business Roundtable participation guide: A primer for business on education.* Washington, DC: Author.

National Association of Partners in Education (NAPE). (1991). *National school district Partnership survey: Statistical report.* Alexandria, Virginia: Author.

National Center for Education Statistics. (1989). *Education partnerships in public elementary and secondary schools.* Washington, DC: United States Department of Education.

Nugent, M. A., & Rigden, D. W. (1994). *Student learning outcomes: One road to school reform.* New York: Council for Aid to Education.

Orlich, D. C. (1989). Education reforms: Mistakes, misconceptions, miscues. *Phi Delta Kappan, 70,* 512–517.

Portner, J. (1995, April 19). *Back to basics: Standards proposals in Virginia under attack.* Education Week, *12*(16), 1–12.

Press, F. (1983, Fall). Commercializing new knowledge. *Educational Horizons, 62,* 3–4.

Ray, C. A., & Mickelson, R. A. (1989). Business leaders and the politics of school reform. In D. Mitchell & M. Goertz (eds.). *Education and politics for the new century* pp. 119–135. New York: Falmer Press.

Reich, R. (1992). *The work of nations.* New York: Vintage Books.

Reingold, J. R. (1990). *Corporate action agenda: The business of improving public education.* Washington, DC: National Alliance of Business.

Rich, W. C. (1996). *Black mayors and school politics: The failure of reform in Detroit, Gary, and Newark.* New York: Garland Publishing.

Southwest Regional Laboratory (1995). *Documentation and evaluation of the educational-partnerships program: Final report.* Los Alamitos, CA: Author.

Timpane, M. (1984). Business has rediscovered the public schools. *Phi Delta Kappan, 65,* 389–392.

United States Department of Labor (USDOL) (1995). *Skills, standards and entry-level work: Elements of a strategy for youth employability development.* (ETA contract No. 99-0-1879-75-053-01). Washington, DC: Author.

part IV
Key Dilemma

9

THE FUTURE OF EDUCATION FINANCE IN IMPROVING PUBLIC EDUCATION

James G. Ward
University of Illinois at Urbana-Champaign

INTRODUCTION

Ellwood P. Cubberley began the preface of his classic book, *School Funds and Their Apportionment*, with these words: "One of the most important administrative problems of to-day is how to properly finance the school system of a state, as the question of sufficient revenues lies back of almost every other problem" (Cubberley, 1905, p. 3). These words are no less true today than they were in the opening years of the 20th century. Although there have been many policy changes over the years, the fact remains that the proper financing of schools is one of the most important administrative and policy questions educators and public policy makers face, and issues of finance are critical to most other educational policy issues.

Historical Background

Through the 19th century and into the early years of the 20th century, the financing of education was largely a local affair, with some state assistance. Local revenue sources for public schools included taxes on real and personal property, rent on public lands, tuition charges, revenues from public enterprises such as mills and ferries, and lottery proceeds in various states and jurisdictions. By the 1870s, rate bills, or tuition charges, had been abandoned in almost all states and the local tax on real property was the main source of public school revenue. As late as 1919 to

1920, public schools in the United States were deriving about 83 percent of their total revenue from local sources, with only 16.5 percent coming in the form of state aid to local districts (United States Department of Education, 1997, p. 157).

Cubberley raised the issue of equalization of education resources within the state in his seminal work and school finance specialists introduced the concept of the foundation formula to help reduce intrastate disparities in per pupil expenditures in the 1920s. As states began to adopt the foundation formula as a mechanism to more equally provide for public education, the state share of total spending rose. Partially in response to pressures for equalization funds and also in response to the economic dislocations of the Great Depression, states in the 1930s instituted state income taxes and state sales taxes and increased their grants-in-aid to local school districts. At the same time, many states abandoned the state tax on real property as a major state revenue source, leaving the real property tax to local governments. By 1939 to 1940, the state share of total public school spending had risen to just over 30 percent, while the local share stood at 68 percent (United States Department of Education, 1997, p. 157).

The fundamental problem in equalization of school resources among districts within a state was identified by Cubberley.

> Theoretically all the children of the state are equally important and are entitled to have the same advantages; practically this can never be quite true. The duty of the state is to secure for all as high a minimum of good instruction as is possible, but not to reduce all to a minimum; to equalize advantages to all as nearly as can be done with the resources at hand; to place a premium on those local efforts which will enable communities to rise above the legal minimum as far as possible; and to encourage communities to extend their educational energies to new and desirable undertakings. (Cubberley, 1905, p. 17)

The conundrum of how to ensure equal educational opportunity for all students has remained with us to this day.

After the Second World War, the rapid expansion of the public school system as a result of the Baby Boom increase in the school-age population shifted the emphasis in school finance policy toward the issue of how to raise adequate resources to fund this burgeoning system. Policy makers worried about how to build enough schools and how to adequately staff them and keep them in supplies and materials. Curriculum reform shifted to the forefront in educational policy circles as we became concerned about the role of public education in the world competition with Communism and the Soviet Union. Funding facilities like science and language laboratories were major issues.

By the 1960s, school desegregation, the Civil Rights Movement, the War on Poverty, and concerns about equal educational opportunity shifted the emphasis in school finance back to equity. By the late 1960s, cases were in first federal and then state courts about the constitutionality of current state school finance systems that allowed tremendous intrastate disparities in public school spending per pupil. Student populations began to fall again after 1972, releasing some fiscal pressures on schools, and the years of the 1970s were the height of the school finance litigation movement. The expansion of programs in special education, compensatory education, bilingual education, and other specials needs programs, however, added to school costs and pressures for increased spending.

Beginning in the early 1980s, schools came under increasing criticism for doing a poor job and, therefore, undermining the competitiveness of the United States in the global marketplace. Emphasis in school finance shifted away from equity toward a concern for adequacy and efficiency in school funding. The question now was not so much how can we provide equitable school funding plans, but how much money should we spend on schools and how should these funds be best used. Even the school finance court cases became less concerned with eliminating intrastate spending disparities and began to emphasize raising the resources spent on education in low-spending districts.

The Current Situation

Public schools receive large amounts of government revenues. According to federal statistics, in 1994 to 1995, public schools in the United States received over $273 billion in revenues (United States Department of Education, 1997). This translated into a current expenditure per pupil of $5,988, a not inconsequential amount. Problems with public school funding do not lie so much with the total amount spent per pupil, but with three related problems.

1. There is a very uneven distribution of dollars spent per pupil. Even disregarding the tremendous disparities that exist within states, the interstate range in current expenditures per pupil went from $3,656 in Utah to $9,774 in New Jersey (United States Department of Education, 1997).
2. There is a clearly articulated dissatisfaction on the parts of many Americans with the performance of public schools. There is a concern that they are not doing their job well and that more money for public schools is not the answer.
3. This is complicated by the fact that public schools have unclear goals. There is great confusion on the part of the public on what precisely are the goals of public schooling and, consequently, how schools should be organized, governed, and funded to reach those goals.

These factors all complicate answering the question about what should be sound school finance policy.

Equity and concerns for social justice in public school finance policy seems to have become less important over the past two decades. A market model of education and education finance seems to have become ascendant. The theme of this chapter is that this has been a movement in the wrong direction and that we need to experience a revival in interest in equity as a policy goal and in social justice in education finance.

SCHOOL FINANCE POLICY: CONFLICTING GOALS

We talk about what concerns us. In the late 1960s and 1970s, "school finance talk" seemed to be about achieving student equity, equal educational opportunity, and social justice. Sometime around 1980, this talk shifted to financing an education to allow the United States to become competitive in global markets, to discussions of producing an adequate supply of "high tech" workers, and to providing incentives for excellence. The conversation changed because goals changed.

Conflicting goals of education finance policy in the United States has resulted from conflicting goals of education itself. Different people simply have different ideas of what they think public education should achieve. We also have very different views about how public education should be governed. Who makes decisions about education policy at the federal, state, and local levels; and how they make education policy, are key factors in determining school finance policy.

One of the prevailing myths in public education policy is that we all share a common vision of the goals of public schools, that is, we all know what public schools are about and what they are supposed to accomplish. James (1991) correctly points out that "education is a contested public good in American society" (p. 169). We do not agree on basic ends, as well as means to achieve those ends, and much conflict in education and educational politics has to do with issues of both ends and means.

The nature of these conflicting goals has been explored by Labaree (1997), who identifies three basic goals of American education that have been in conflict with one another over the years: *democratic equality*, *social efficiency*, and *social mobility*.

In the goal of democratic equality, Labaree "sees schools as an expression of democratic political ideals and as a mechanism for preparing children to play constructive roles in a democratic society" (Labaree, 1997, p. 43). This goal focuses on preparing citizens in a democratic society and emphasizes citizenship training, equal treatment, and equal access. It is from this tradition that we see public schools as instruments of equal educational opportunity and serving the needs of all children. In school finance policy, the goal of democratic equality provides the foundation for the movements toward student equity in funding and programs and school finance reform litigation.

The educational goal of social efficiency has "sought to make schools a mechanism for adapting students to the requirements of a hierarchical social structure and the demands of the occupational marketplace" (Labaree, 1997, p. 46). This goal has been operationalized, according to Labaree, through vocationalism and educational stratification in schools. Schools exist to provide the human capital needs of society. Clearly, many business leaders in the United States see social efficiency as the paramount goal of public education. In public school finance policy, social efficiency undergirds interest in accountability, competition, and privatization of schooling.

Finally, social mobility, as a goal of education, "argues that schools should adapt students to the existing socioeconomic structure, the social mobility goal asserts that schools should provide students with the educational credentials they need in order to get ahead in this structure (or to maintain their current position)" (Labaree, 1997, p. 50). Here, the focus is on individual *status attainment* and on understanding that the benefits of education are to be *selective* and *differential*, with extensive stratification of schools and programs. Public schools in affluent suburban communities and elite private schools are manifestations of the goal of social mobility. In school finance policy, social mobility is reflected in an emphasis on adequacy and resistance to movements toward student equity.

These goals are all present in current debates on educational policy and on public school finance policy. They commonly come in conflict with one another and contribute to the fact that education is very much a contested good in the American political arena. As Labaree (1997) concludes:

> One obvious effect of these three goals has been to create within American education a structure that is contradictory and frequently counterproductive. In response to the various demands put on them, educational institutions are simultaneously moving in a variety of directions that are often in opposition to one another. . . . As a result of being forced to muddle it goals and continually work at cross-purposes, education inevitably turns out to be deficient in carrying out any of these goals very effectively." (pp. 70–71)

The movement from emphasis on democratic equality in the 1960s and 1970s to the growing domination of social mobility as a goal has been reflected in school finance by the movement away from equity toward adequacy as a policy goal. Public schools may be better funded than they were two decades ago, but they certainly are not more equitably funded. An important question is the degree of permanence of this value shift. One of the critical issues for public school finance policy for the opening years of the 21st century is whether and to what extent we might return to a stronger emphasis on democratic equality.

A FRAMEWORK FOR CONSIDERING
SCHOOL FINANCE POLICY ISSUES

Public school finance policy differences are based on differing views of how the world works and value differences. A number of value and world view issues provide a framework for consideration of public school finance policy.

Education: Private Good or Social Good?

An overarching issue, which affects educational finance, governance, and administration is the question of whether we view public education in the United States as a social good or a private good? Of course, we recognize that education benefits both the individual and the community, so education is both a social good and a private good. The policy question, however, centers on which receives the greater emphasis.

If education is regarded largely as a private good, the benefits of which accrue to the individual, then education should be provided through the market. In today's political climate, this would be largely an unregulated market. Educational vouchers, charter schools, and tuition tax credits are variations on this theme.

One commentary on the movement toward school choice has described the debate so far as largely centering around what mechanisms will work best to provide competition within a market system to improve K–12 education. The real issue, however, is "Those who debate the pros and cons of school choice have missed the central point. Parents want to send their children to schools that are free *not* to teach all children" [emphasis in original] (McGhan, 1998, p. 610).

Parents often desire choice so that they may place their children in schools not attended by children who the parents feel to be undesirable for whatever reason. Those deemed undesirable may be so because of behavior, academic ability, academic interest, socioeconomic class, gender, religion, or race. The interest of those favoring school choice clearly comes down on the side of education as a private good by favoring an exclusionary policy that denies some children whatever benefits of choice there might be. As legal scholars remind us, every time we include, we exclude (Minow, 1990). It is by exclusion that we satisfy the requirements of social efficiency and social mobility.

If, on the other hand, education is regarded as a social good, the primary benefit of education accruing to society, then education should be provided through the polity, or the political community, through public budgets in public institutions. This means including everyone in a public system that guarantees equal educational opportunity along the lines of the values of democratic equality.

This debate is a current and lively one, and one not likely to be resolved in the near future. How one regards these issues and how one views education, however, will have a profound effect on the approach to school finance policy.

Equity or Adequacy?

A second large issue is to what extent is student equity still a paramount goal, or has it been replaced by adequacy? Are we willing to allow large variations in per pupil expenditure across districts if we can be assured that every child has at least a threshold level of funding, or are large variations in student spending unacceptable under any circumstances? Are students, in general, better off in New York State, with its large intrastate disparities, but generally high level of spending, or in Kentucky, with smaller intrastate disparities and a fairly low level of spending? (Parrish & Hikido, 1998).

In many states in the 1980s and 1990s, school finance reform changed radically from trying to eliminate disparities in per pupil spending across school districts within a state to a policy of bring the bottom half of the per pupil spending distribution up to some middle point and allowing the school districts in the high spending half of the distribution to continue their past practices unrestrained. This threshold principle allows one portion of schools to focus on some level of minimum adequacy and allows the more affluent districts to continue large disparities in per pupil spending.

Some school finance pundits have proclaimed that "equity is dead." Is it dead or simply dormant? Will democratic equality ever again become the dominant value in public education?

Efficiency and the Schools

A third major issue is the question of the efficient use of school resources. How can education revenues be used more efficiently? Does money make a difference? How does money make a difference?

Business values and a strong emphasis on efficiency in school operations held definite sway in the first four decades of the 20th century (Callahan, 1962). Those demanding greater efficiency in the operation of American schools are fond of citing literature that argues that no additional investment of money in public schools will produce improved results. The research, however, has not always been that clear.

Recent research has shown that high quality teachers and administrators seem to have the greatest impact on increased student performance. Political commentator E. J. Dionne Jr. concluded a column on the subject by writing:

> Americans value both a fair shake for all and an emphasis on education and achievement. It turns out that bringing the two together may be the most promising road to racial and social justice. Give kids good teachers, and amazing things happen. (Dionne, 1998)

So, a question that must be addressed is how do we provide good teachers for all children. Among the issues to be addressed, and one that school finance policy must consider, is how do we create conditions to attract and retain the best possible personnel for our public schools? Part of the issue relates to professional standards and reasonable conditions of work and another aspect is to determine how to create compensation systems to attract and retain high quality teachers and administrators.

A related efficiency question is do we target federal and state funds for fairly narrow purposes to achieve clear goals of increased performance in selected areas, or do we provide funds in block grants and leave the efficient use of those resources up to the judgment of local officials? Targeted funds may ensure investment of resources in programs deemed to be most efficient or effective, but narrow targeting may stifle local initiative and create inefficiencies in local districts and schools. Block grants allow local officials to makes decisions about the best use of funds, but those choices may differ from the policy objectives of the state or federal funders.

To what extent will demands for greater accountability and increased use of state revenue sources for public education reduce local control and lead to centralization of governance and financing of schools? The movement toward federal and state standards and greater accountability of local school officials is a clear threat to local control, a value which is sacred to many policy makers. There is a built-in contradiction between increased system accountability and maximum local discretion in policy making.

These questions also involve important governance questions around the issues of centralization and local control. These are volatile political questions that certainly affect funding policies.

Shifting Education Need

How do we face the challenge of shifting educational need? A number of state school systems are becoming minority-majority systems. Today, urban school systems, suburban school systems, and rural districts look less alike than they have probably ever looked before. The gulf between the "haves" and "have-nots" seems to be increasing, with a widening gulf in inequality in incomes and pay in the United States (Galbraith, 1998). We know how to successfully educate poor children and minority children, but are we willing to pay the price? Will we invest sufficient funds, for example, in urban districts to create equal educational opportunity and improved student performance, or will we slowly dismantle urban public education through school choice and vouchers? In many states, we are seeing the "politics of privilege," where the affluent protect themselves through high quality public schools or public assistance for private schools and urban school districts and districts with high incidence of children from families in poverty go begging. The protectors of privilege oppose school finance reform, whether pursued through the legislative process or through the courts. These kinds of policy choices will have a direct impact on school finance policies in the future.

Revenues for Public Schools

Finally, we have the issue of revenue sources. Cubberley (1905) raised the issue of sufficient revenues for public schools. A significant policy question is what should be the sources for those revenues. This question involves the level of government—federal, state, and local—that should be the major source of revenues, as well as the type of tax that should fund public schools. In many states there is interest in replacing real property tax revenues for public schools with some state source of revenue, such as state income tax revenues or state sales tax revenues. State lottery and gambling tax revenues are part of the mix in many states, although there is an increasing realization that these sources may not be as stable as once thought. State fiscal policy for education is complex and these issues are not simple. Many states are watching Michigan to see how their "grand experiment" in school finance works, which substituted state revenue sources for local property tax revenues in a complex redistribution plan that moved toward both student and taxpayer equity. The tentative answer is that all is not well in Michigan and the current system may be just a temporary interlude. This remains to be seen.

This framework for public school finance policy has attempted to raise some of the larger policy issues that have an impact on how we finance public schools.

SCHOOL FINANCE POLICY IN THE 1990S

Based on events and trends of the 1990s and a scan of the various states, we can identify a number of future directions or questions about school finance policy that will likely determine policy decisions. These indicate actual policy directions from the framework discussed previously.

In the 1980s and 1990s, there was a clear retreat from concerns about student equity and an increased interest in student adequacy. This was demonstrated in a number of state school finance reform cases where the emphasis was not on equal protection, but on the education article of the state constitution and concerns about the adequacy of educational programs. The goals were not on achieving greater equity in student spending, but on raising the funding level of low spending districts. The difference is important.

There also was a heightened interest in resource allocation issues. In the light of research that has supposedly shown that money does not make a difference in education, researchers and policy makers have regarded education spending as a social investment and have sought to better understand how resources can be allocated in schools to produce greater student performance. The question has shifted from does money make a difference to how does money make a difference.

There has been an interest in various privatization or quasi-privatization policy mechanisms has increased. This has manifested itself in policy initiatives like vouchers for low-income, inner-city youth, charter schools, home schooling, de-regulation of high performing schools (often in affluent suburban areas), and outright calls for the elimination of the public school system and dependence on private schools. These proposals all share a view that the individual benefit of education is dominant over the social benefit and that social benefit can be maximized through the aggregation of private benefits.

Finally, national political and social policies have influenced state and local political culture and have had an effect on schools and education funding. The emphasis on a balanced federal budget and on smaller government has constrained federal social policies and programs, including education. Anti-tax sentiment and cynicism about government have made education funding increases more difficult to achieve. Rhetoric extolling the virtues of the free market has increased interest in private sector alternatives to the public school.

THE FUTURE OF EDUCATION FINANCE
IN THE UNITED STATES

How will school finance fare over the next decade and how will other factors influence education finance policy in the United States? Some of the factors that are critical are:

- Changing demographics in the United States; the emergence of "minority-majority" states in terms of school enrollment; the rising Hispanic student population in states like California, Texas, Florida, Illinois, and New York; and the increasing incidence of poverty among children. Near record levels of immigration, with immigrants often concentrated in a few states or metropolitan areas, is adding pressures for increased educational services in many districts.
- The increasing demand for educational services stemming from increasing student enrollments in many states and the increasing demands on education from a global, information-based economy, as well as from increased use of technology in the workplace.
- The culture of contentment and the move toward the protection of privilege by the affluent in our society and related factors such as the growth of exurbia and edge cities, the increasing income gap in the United States, privatization in education, and the dominance of the free market philosophy.
- The future of the balanced budget movement, fiscal restraint, and its effect on social policies and the federal social safety net.
- The relation of school finance systems to issues such as student standards and assessment, coordinated social services for children, and welfare reform.

CONCLUSION

Education policy is often dependent on larger social movements in the United States and on social, economic, and political trends. We cannot simply extrapolate current trends into future predictions, but we can speculate on how some of these issues will emerge in the future.

The globalization of the economy and the increased use of technology in all aspects of daily life may well support a greater emphasis on the individual and the lessened importance of a geographically based community. This may foster an continuing trend toward individualism, education as a private good, and increased support for using an unregulated market to allocate education through charter schools, vouchers, and the privatization of education. This does not bode well for the proponents of democratic quality and it may mean the end of universal public education, particularly in the cities. We may emerge with a bifurcated education system with high quality public schools in affluent areas and in less affluent areas, we may find a system of high quality private and charter schools for the affluent and substandard, underfunded public schools for the poor.

Events of the last two decades, starting with the tax revolts of the late 1970s and early 1980s and continuing through the balanced budget culture of the 1990s, indicate that there will be no cessation in the trend towards lower taxes, smaller government, and opposition to governmental expenditures, except in the areas of income security, old age pensions (Social Security), and government support for business. Expenditures for public education, especially in cities and poor school districts, will be increasing characterized as consumption rather than investment. The aging Baby Boomers will provide lessened support for increasing taxes for public schools, as they struggle to maintain their standard of living as they approach and move into retirement.

The culture of individualism and unregulated free markets will prevail. The Internet "chat room" rather than the local PTA meeting will become the norm of social interaction on policy matters. Loyalties will lie less in the local community than they will with people of similar education, economic status, culture, and profession across the globe. Democratic equality will continue to fall to the notion of allocation of goods and services through competition in the market. "I am my brother's keeper" will fall victim to "Why isn't my brother competitive?" One historian has termed this the "revolt of the elites" (Lasch, 1995).

School finance policy will turn its attention increasingly to issues of how to devise financial incentive systems to reward performance, how to fund charter schools and charter school districts, the financing of technology, the provision of education by private systems through public funding, and performance-based compensation systems.

This scenario could change if our political culture returns to an earlier concern for racial and social justice or if the pressures for racial and social justice become so great that there is serious disruption in the order of American life. Some have suggested that just as the protests and urban riots of the 1960s helped bring about serious social change in the 1960s, that a similar "revolt of the have-nots" could alter the scenario presented here. School finance policy would certainly be affected by this.

A return to equity as the major policy goal in education is not likely, but if we are to maintain a public education system that serves all children well, then we have no choice but to reemphasize equity and equal educational opportunity. The allocation of educational services based on free market fundamentalism will serve a few well, but will ill serve the commonwealth.

REFERENCES

Callahan, R. E. (1962). *Education and the cult of efficiency: A study of the social forces that have shaped the administration of public schools.* Chicago: University of Chicago Press.

Cubberley, E. P. (1905). *School funds and their apportionment.* New York: Columbia University.

Dionne, E. J., Jr. (1998). Good teachers do make a difference. *Washington Post National Weekly Edition,* August 18, 1998, p. 32.

Galbraith, J. K. (1998). *Created unequal: The crisis in American pay.* New York: Free Press.

James, T. (1991). State authority and the politics of educational change. In G. Grant (Ed.), *Review of Research in Education 17* (pp. 169–224). Washington, DC: American Educational Research Association.

Labaree, D. F. (1997). Public goods, private goods: The American struggle over educational goals. *American Educational Research Journal, 34,* 39–81.

Lasch, C. (1995). *The revolt of the elites and the betrayal of democracy.* New York: Norton.

McGhan, B. (1998). Choice and compulsion: The end of an era. *Phi Delta Kappan, 79,* 610–612.

Minow, M. (1990). *Making all the difference: Inclusion, exclusion, and the American law.* Ithaca: Cornell University Press.

Parrish, T. B., & Hikido, C. S. (1998). *Inequalities in public school district revenues* (NCES 98-210). Washington DC: United States Department of Education.

United States Department of Education. (1997). *Digest of educational statistics* (Publication No. NCES 98-015). Washington, DC: United States Government Printing Office.

10

THE SCHOOL LEADERSHIP SHORTAGE: FRAMEWORK FOR POLICY DISCUSSION

Bruce Anthony Jones
University of Missouri

School systems across the nation are faced with varying and significant school leadership problems. Not too long ago, school principalships were highly sought positions. Today in many areas of the country, these positions go unfilled, or school districts are faced with fewer choices from shrinking candidate pools (Armstrong, 1990; Olson, 1999). At last count, the average tenure of an urban superintendent was 6 years (Domenech, 1996). These school leadership problems are exacerbated by the fact that women and members of ethnic minority groups are not adequately represented among the ranks of school superintendents and principals (Hodgkinson & Montenegro, 1999; Keller, 1998a; Tallerico, Burstyn, & Poole, 1993). Few policy strategies have been crafted or employed to address this fact. Moreover, little empirical research has been done to determine the reasons why the school leadership problem developed and why it persists. There are, however, numerous anecdotes and "gut" feelings about the problem (Gmelch, 1996). The dearth of research in the area of the school leadership problem has made it difficult to begin to develop policy solutions.

On November 16, 1998, the National Policy Board in Educational Administration *Policy Circle* (NPBEA Policy Circle)[1] convened a national meeting to address the school leadership problem. The meeting was held in Denver, Colorado, at the offices of the Education Commission of the States. Attendees included school superintendents, principals, representatives of national education associations, university academicians, school board members, and representatives of the philanthropic community. The discussions at the Denver meeting guide much of the content of this chapter.

THE "SENSE" OF URGENCY

Over the past decade, there has been a continuing national trend toward growing school administrator shortages. In a national survey administered by the National Association of Elementary School Principals (1998) and the National Association of Secondary School Principals, over half of the superintendent respondents reported significant shortages in the supply of candidates for school principalships. Moreover, according to the United States Bureau of Labor Statistics there is a projected 10 to 20 percent increase in administrator job vacancies overall expected by the year 2005 (Keller, 1998a).

Little has been done in a systematic way at a policy level to ward off the trend described previously. "Anecdotal" information appears to be all that policy makers have as a justification for beginning to address the school leadership shortage. In the absence of empirical data, several reasons for the school administrator shortage have been cited in the literature. These reasons include the aging of the administrator cohort (Bowles, 1990; McCormick, 1987) and an undersupply of qualified educators willing to pursue administrator positions. Moreover, there is evidence that administrators are leaving public education in response to stress and demands caused by difficult day-to-day problems and responsibilities (Abrell, 1984; Keller, 1998b; McCormick, 1987; Pawlas, 1989; Trotter, 1999). Administrators also complain of growing and unnecessary paperwork and documentation (Pawlas, 1989) mandated as a part of their administrative responsibilities. The paperwork requirements mean that they have less time to focus on students and curriculum matters. Early retirement inducements (Bowles, 1990; McCormick, 1987), and, in some cases, the lack of job security in entry-level administrative positions (Bowles, 1990) also may contribute to reported school administrator shortages.

Bowles (1990) reports that the undersupply of school administrators is exacerbated on the front-end of the administrative profession, as fewer young teachers are choosing careers in administration. Moreover, women and members of ethnic minority groups have not entered the administrative workforce at the expected rates, which is especially perplexing in the case of women, who currently constitute more than half of those completing school administration programs (Bowles, 1990; Johnson, 1987; Shakeshaft, 1998).

WHO WANTS AND WHO GETS THIS JOB?

According to a study conducted on the profile of the superintendent in the United States, approximately 88 percent are male. Figure 10.1 illustrates that the number

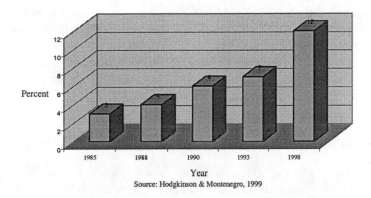

Year

Source: Hodgkinson & Montenegro, 1999

FIGURE 10.1.   Women in the superintendency.

TABLE 10.1.
Gender of Public School Principals

Gender	Percent
Male	65.4
Female	34.5

Note: Details may not add to 100 percent due to rounding.

Source: United States Department of Education, NCES (1997).

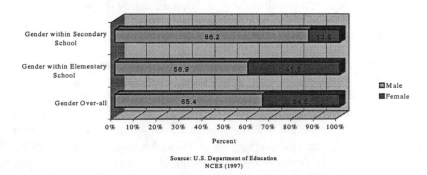

Percent

Source: U.S. Department of Education
NCES (1997)

FIGURE 10.2.   Percentage of public school principals by gender and school level 1993 to 1994.

of women in the superintendency grew four-fold between 1985 and 1998. In 1985, approximately 3 percent of all superintendents were female. This grew to approximately 12 percent by 1998 (Hodgkinson & Montenegro, 1999). A report by the United States Department of Education (NCES) (1997) revealed that as of 1994, men comprised approximately 65.4 percent of all school principalships (Table 10.1). Figure 10.2 shows that most principalships held by women continue to be predominantly at the elementary school level.

THE SHORTAGE AND OVERALL CONTRIBUTING FACTORS

The administrator shortage dilemma appears to be divisible under two broad "policy implication" discussion areas. Figures 10.3 and 10.4 provide these discussion areas. The first discussion area, *internal development factors*, is concerned with issues that surround recruitment, selection, retention, preparation, and ongoing leadership training in the profession (Figure 10.3). The second area, *external development factors*, concerns the relationship between schools, school districts, and the community at large (Figure 10.4).

Internal Development Factors

In the national survey and follow-up interviews that were administered to a sample of school superintendents across the country by the National Association of Elementary School Principals and the National Association of Secondary School Principals, the two most significant factors that were cited as inhibiting superintendents from recruiting applicants for the principalship were *job stress* (32% of the interview respondents) and *inadequate salary compensation* (60% of interview respondents) associated with the position of the principalship. These factors were combined with the view that the principalship is too demanding, with too much pressure associated with public scrutiny and accountability (Figure 10.5).

Is the Profession an Occupational Hazard?

Without question, the job of the superintendent and school principal has become more stressful in recent years. Beginning most recently with the *effective schools* research, principals were cited as the most significant individuals in a school building. This research reveals over and over again that the leadership capability of school principals determines whether or not a school fails or succeeds. The public pressure on school principals to perform well is exacerbated by the growth in job duties. According to Olson (1999): "[Principals] are expected not only to be instructional leaders but also disciplinarians, supervisors, fund-raisers, public relations experts, and fiscal managers. They have to worry about liability concerns as well as who picks up the garbage" (p. 2). Using Texas as an example, Keller (1998a)

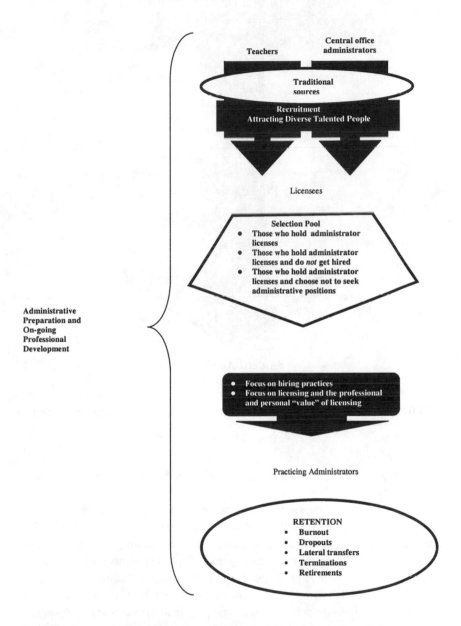

FIGURE 10.3. Administrative shortage dilemma, internal development factors.

Source: Forsyth & Jones, 1998.

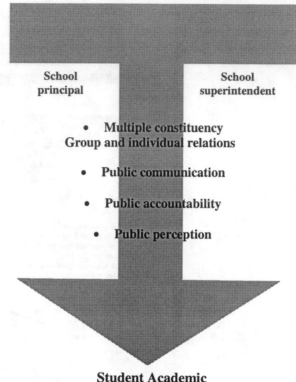

School
principal

School
superintendent

- Multiple constituency
Group and individual relations

- Public communication

- Public accountability

- Public perception

**Student Academic
Achievement**

FIGURE 10.4. Administrative shortage dilemma, external development factors.

reports, "there's not a hotter seat in all of education than the one in the principal's office" (p. 1).

For superintendents, the situation is not much better. Superintendents engage in numerous job responsibilities that include implementation of school board policy, curriculum planning, collective bargaining, finance planning, personnel hiring, termination, and human resource development. Superintendents must be accountable to federal and state regulations. They must engage in facilities management tasks and build relationships with school board members, taxpayers, parents, personnel throughout the school system, and people in the community at large.

According to a study by Tallerico, Poole, & Burstyn (1994), superintendents reported several instances whereby the job was too political. School board members often were more interested in the "politicization of superintendents' work" (p. 444) than education matters as this relates to caring about the children. In the current

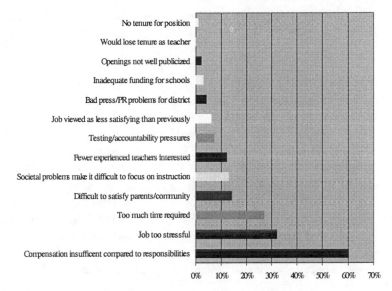

Source: National Association of Elementary School Principals (1998).

FIGURE 10.5.   What discourages applicants?

environment, Chand (1990) provides a sampling of what it is like to be a school superintendent.

- In 1990, the superintendent of Prince George's County pulled out of his contract. "Racial politics and political gamesmanship" were given as his reasons for departure.
- The breakdown in the relations between the superintendent of Boston public schools and the community led to the buy-out of his contract for $260,000 in 1990.
- In 1990, the superintendent of Columbus, Ohio was almost ousted as a result of conflict with African American community groups, only 16 months into his 3-year contract.
- In 1989, a superintendent in California was shot as he left the school district office.
- In 1985, the superintendent of Cleveland, Ohio schools committed suicide after leaving a suicide note complaining about the school board's "petty politics."
- The superintendent of schools in Vader, Washington reported he "just ran away" from the pressure of the job.
- In Newark, New Jersey the school board awarded a settlement of $660,000 to the superintendent to render his resignation. This occurred in 1985.

■ The superintendent of Matanuska-Susitna Borough School District in Alaska was provided a settlement of $185,000 by the board of education to "get out of town."

As far back as 1954, Spaulding (1954) reported, "superintendents have more anxiety than any other people who I have tested outside of mental institutions" (p. 1). As recently as 1999, three candidates for the superintendency of the Kansas City, Missouri public schools (in succession) entered into final contract negotiations with the school board. All three pulled out of the negotiations when they witnessed the gross incompetence of the school board. One of the candidates reported, "the prospects of being cast in an adversarial role so early in my relationship with this (school) board is not one that I relish or am willing to contemplate." According to the Mayor of Kansas City: "This [superintendent] search is a national embarrassment. . . . anyone who takes the job under the current conditions will not succeed" (O'Connor & Stearns, 1999, p. 1).

With regard to both positions (the principalship and superintendency), Houston (1998) reports,

One of my first experiences as a new principal was learning to live with seeing my name mentioned in the newspaper in less than flattering descriptions . . . (as superintendent a board member reminded) me that my job was to be a *quick healing dartboard*.

More attention will be needed to research on the "health" of school administrators (Torelli & Gmelch, 1993). In what ways can the "health" of school administrators become incorporated as a permanent concern in discussions about school reform, administrative preparation, and professional development? Do school administrators suffer from mental and physical illness (i.e., heart attacks, strokes, and cancer) more than others who serve in similar occupational roles? Studies already document the comparatively high levels of stress experienced by women and ethnic minorities in the labor market (Light, et al., 1995; Willie, et al., 1995). Could this be a contributing factor that explains the low presence of women and ethnic minorities in the school administrative profession? Are the responsibilities associated with these positions too numerous and complex for one individual?

Compensation

The salary compensation issue is intertwined with the stress factors previously listed. According to Hess (1988), superintendents and school principals repeatedly report that they are undervalued relative to the job responsibilities they hold. Superintendent and school principal salaries are extremely low when compared with the salaries of chief executive officers in private industry. Moreover:

No job—even one as noble as school administration—justifies the long hours of frustrations involved in dealing with red tape, political obstacles, and the demands of constituents who accost them on the street with complaints about their child's bus route or classroom assignment. (p. 44)

Table 10.2 provides the average annual salaries of school principals and super-intendents during 1997 to 1998.

Preparation and Professional Development

The preparation of potential school administrators and ongoing professional development of practicing administrators are critical factors to include in policy-related discussion on current school administrator shortages. In this respect, a number of questions emerge with regard to what is believed that prospective school administrators need to know and how to assess proficiency levels of practicing school administrators. Closely related to the latter is the question of how to determine whether or not administrators are competent enough to retain their jobs.

An analysis of the 1991–1996 editions of the *Manual on Certification and Preparation of Educational Personnel in the United States* revealed that over a 5-year period, approximately 19 states made changes in administrative licensure requirements. These changes occurred as part of a policy effort to address the questions raised in the preceding paragraph. More specifically: (1) seven states added, changed, or ceased using a specific administrative examination requirement; (2) two states added an administrative examination requirement; (3) four states implemented some form of performance-based assessment; (4) four states changed the term of the initial license; (5) two states changed the required amount of teaching experience required; and (6) two states changed the length of the administrative internship. According to Crawford (1998), between 1991 and 1996 at least six states added performance-based assessment as a method for evaluating the competencies of (already licensed) practicing administrators.

The influence of national reform standards on administrative preparation and professional development programs is growing. For example, the Interstate Lead-

TABLE 10.2.
Principals and Superintendents Salaries (1997–1998)

Position	Average Annual Salary
Superintendents	$101,519
Elementary school principal	$64,653
Middle school principal	$68,740
High school principal	$74,380

Source: United States Department of Education, NCES (1997).

ership Licensure Consortium (ISLC) examination has been adopted in 25 states by state education agencies. The principles that guide the standards for the examination are directly linked to national education reform standards. These principles are:

- Standards should reflect the centrality of student learning.
- Standards should acknowledge the changing role of the school leader.
- Standards should recognize the collaborative nature of school leadership.
- Standards should be high, upgrading the quality of the profession.
- Standards should inform performance-based systems of assessment and evaluation for school leaders.
- Standards should be integrated and coherent. (Murphy, 1999)

Figure 10.6 provides the ISLC framework for discussion and adoption of these principles.

University-based educational leadership preparation programs are often criticized for being too theoretical in the curriculum orientation and out of touch with the day-to-day "real" experiences of a school leader. As a way to address this criticism in part, some university-based preparation programs have also adopted the ISLC framework for changing the instruction and curriculum (Murphy, 1999).

Multiple institutions are involved with influencing the administrative preparation and professional development of school administrators. These institutions include state education agencies, university-based preparation programs, national professional associations, and, to a lesser (but growing) degree, the federal government.

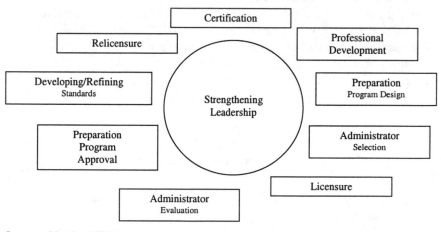

Source: Murphy (1999)

FIGURE 10.6.   Interstate school leaders licensure consortium standards: framework for action.

Given this, there needs to be concern about program coordination, competing interests, and contradictory information about what is believed that school administrators should know and how they should be held accountable.

Ethnic Minority and Female Outlook: Ongoing Saga

Members of ethnic minority groups (American Indian/Alaska Native, Asian/Pacific Islander, African American, and Hispanic American) are woefully under-represented among the ranks of the superintendency and principalship. Insofar as the superintendency is concerned, little change occurred with ethnic minority representation between 1985 and 1998 (Figure 10.7). In 1985, only 3 percent of all superintendent posts were held by members of ethnic minority groups. Over the next 13 years this remained relatively unchanged. By 1998, only 5 percent of all superintendent posts were held by members of ethnic minority groups (Hodgkinson & Montenegro, 1999). At the principalship level, Table 10.3 shows that 84.2 percent of all principalships are held by European Americans.

The increase in the number of women who served in school principalships was supported by data results from a 1998 survey conducted by the National Association of Elementary School Principals and the National Association of Secondary School Principals. The respondents to the survey were school superintendents who in general revealed little difficulty with recruitment efforts aimed at women. Respondents did reveal that there was difficulty with the recruitment and selection of members of ethnic minority groups. Approximately 17 percent of the respondents indicated difficulty with increasing the number of "women in management positions" in their districts compared with 35 percent who indicated difficulty with increasing the number of "minorities" in their districts.

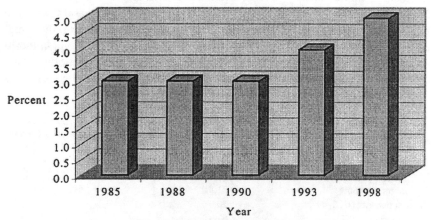

Source: Hodgkinson & Montenegro(1999)

FIGURE 10.7. Ethnic minorities in the superintendency.

TABLE 10.3.
Ethnicity of Public School Principals

Ethnicity	Percentage
American Indian/Alaskan Native	0.8
Asian/Pacific Islander	0.8
African American non-Hispanic	10.1
European American non-Hispanic	84.2
Hispanic	4.1
Total Minority	15.7

Note: Details may not add to 100 percent due to rounding.

Source: United States Department of Education, NCES (1997).

The lack of recruitment and selection of members of ethnic minority groups will have dire consequences for schools and school districts in the future in a demographic and ethical sense. As of 1998, 33 percent of all public school students are members of ethnic minority groups. By the year 2025, European American students will no longer comprise the majority of pubic school enrollees in the United States (Hodgkinson & Montenegro, 1999). From this demographic standpoint, school leaders will increasingly need to reflect the ethnic make-up of the communities they are to lead. This is also a vital consideration if schools are to work toward building bridges and *credibility* in the communities where they are domiciled. On a closely related matter, a double standard continues to exist with regard to the high number of European Americans who hold leadership positions in school districts that are predominantly ethnic minority. The reverse is seldom true, however, that is, members of ethnic minority groups who hold leadership posts in school districts that are predominantly European American. Table 10.4 reveals that the relatively few principalships held by members of ethnic minority groups occur only in high minority enrolled school districts. Approximately 11.1 percent of ethnic minority principals serve in schools with high European American student enrollment and low ethnic minority enrollment whereas approximately 30 percent of the principal-

TABLE 10.4.
Percentage of Minority Principals Working in Public Schools With Varying Levels of Minority Enrollments 1990–1991

Demographics	Percent of Public Schools	Percent of Minority Principals
High minority (≥ 50%)	21.8	69.3
Medium minority (< 20–49%)	20.9	19.6
Low minority (< 20%)	57.3	11.1

Source: United States Department of Education, NCES (1997).

ship positions in high minority schools with low European American student enrollment are held by European Americans.

The Informal Dynamic

There is a growing body of literature that centers on the significance of the need to better understand and deal with the *informal dynamic* of the administrative recruitment and selection process in public education, and how this dynamic may undermine policies aimed at increasing the number of women and ethnic minorities in school administrative posts (Feistritzer, 1988; Hudson, 1994; Tallerico, Burstyn, & Poole, 1993; Tallerico, Poole, & Burstyn, 1994). Hudson (1994) writes "an investigation into the use of informal job contacts in educational administration would seem to offer new perspectives as to why some school administrators are able to get jobs and others are not" (p. 387).

For discussion here, the *informal dynamic* in the job market may manifest in an intentional or unintentional way through a double standard of practice that is applied differentially to individual job seekers based on gender and ethnicity. One standard places emphasis on *who you know*. With this standard, the decision on whether or not to grant employment is overly dominated by the personal connections or social networks of the individual job seeker. According to Hudson (1994) "regardless of competency or merit, those without the right (social/informal) contacts are penalized in the job market. Sixty-two percent of all school superintendents learn about their jobs through informal contacts" (p. 387). The classic "old boy network" (predominantly European American males) serves as an example (Feistritzer, 1988). Members of "old boy networks" forge relations outside of formal professional settings and exchange information about career advancement opportunities in a way that is not available to others (predominantly women and ethnic minorities) who are not members.

The social networks described also serve to perpetuate the myth that males are natural born leaders. The issue about whether or not males (as a group) are "qualified" to hold leadership positions is a nonissue. The issue about who is "qualified" for leadership positions more likely arises around discussions of women (as a group) and members of ethnic minorities (as a group). In other words, males as a category of people are automatically viewed favorably for leadership roles until they prove otherwise. This automatic thinking does not occur for women and ethnic minority groups. In a study by Tallerico and associates (1993), the survey results of 24 female superintendents revealed how adversely they were treated (professionally and personally) because of the perception that school leadership positions were "a man's job" (p. 10).

The myths about the leadership capabilities of people based on gender and ethnic group categories come into play when discussions ensue about individual female and individual ethnic minority applicants who seek leadership positions and whether or not they are "technically qualified" for these positions. In this instance, for individual women and individual members of ethnic minority groups, the other standard of the informal dynamic (what you know) is more often rigidly adhered to. The what you know standard demands a heavy emphasis on the concept of *meritocracy* in the job hiring process. A meritocracy assumes that there is total *objectivity* in the job hiring process. In a meritocracy, professional degrees, experience, and technical expertise of the job applicant are of utmost importance. Several authors have written about the *myth of the meritocracy*.[2] The notion of meritocracy ignores the significance of the *subjective* nature of the job hiring process. The notion ignores the existence of negative group perceptions that are directed toward individual women and ethnic minorities as this relates to leadership capability and potential. It is not automatically accepted that these individuals will have "the look" or "what it takes" to serve in leadership roles. Furthermore, the who you know standard discussed earlier diminishes the credibility of the notion that there is a pure meritocracy operating at any level of the labor force.

Institutions that may intentionally and unintentionally sustain the informal dynamic that precludes women and members of ethnic minority groups from securing what are considered senior level school administrative posts include state school board associations, university professors in educational administration programs, and superintendent associations. These institutions play a central role in determining who actually secures school principalships and superintendencies. Hudson (1994) reports that the negative impact of these networks are more likely to be diluted in instances where women and members of ethnic minority groups are represented on decision-making boards or organizations that hire school leaders. Furthermore, significant change is not expected in this area unless policies are crafted that systematically and directly address the issue.

If there is to be a serious concern with the inadequate supply of women and members of ethnic minorities in school administrative positions it is critically necessary to analyze the informal dynamic and how this operates in the job recruitment, selection, and retention process. This policy-related research will need to be concerned with gender (male and female) and ethnic (all ethnic groups) career mobility as this relates to: (1) how individuals are socialized, coached, and actively mentored into leadership positions; (2) decision-makers who are in critical roles that determine (ultimately) the fate of who gets what employment position and when; (3) historic patterns of racism and sexism (overall discrimination); and (4) how this comes into play around issues of "who" is considered "qualified" to hold administrative leadership posts.

Education and Community Building

The relationship between school leaders and the public has undergone enormous change in recent years. According to Goodlad (1984), from an education standpoint, we live in an *educational ecosystem* whereby numerous institutions and individual players within a given community are integrally interdependent. Public schools do not operate in a vacuum. From an academic standpoint, student achievement is tied to the experiences of the student in and outside the school. Therefore, there has been the growing realization that schools cannot raise academic standards and student achievement without support from the larger community. Education reform strategies must include a school–community focus. From a resource acquisition standpoint, public schools cannot operate in isolation. In an age of diminishing support and skepticism toward public schools, administrators have had to adopt *entrepreneurial strategies*[3] for raising resources to support basic school functions. This requires leadership that fosters creative ways to solicit support for public education from institutions in the community. Institutions and leaders associated with these institutions can no longer act independently or execute decisions unilaterally devoid of the inclusion of *multiple constituencies* in the community (Jones, 1994). These multiple constituencies include parents of children who are enrolled in public education; increasingly, taxpayers who have no children enrolled in the school system; business; higher education; philanthropy; and the mass media.

The public accountability trend is advanced by the bottom-line, that is student achievement. School leaders are faced with the realization that formal education is growing in significance as this relates to the masses of children in the United States. Outside of a quality public education there are fewer routes to becoming a productive citizen. Children who are not properly educated will not likely succeed in society. In the world economy as it is and is becoming, school leaders will have to do more than simply raise student learning and achievement to a *tolerable level of adequacy.*

With the changes in the economy alluded to above, school systems that do not excel will clearly face some sort of external pressure to change. For example, in New York City the mayor recently called for the removal of one third of all school principals in the system at the elementary school level. According to Hartocollis (1999), more than 200 principals could lose their jobs. Earlier, 109 schools in Chicago were put on probation because of unacceptable school failure (McLaughlin, 1998). Across the country in urban school settings, mayors are moving toward attempts to take on failing school districts (White, 1999). Educational alternatives to traditional forms of education and school governance are growing. Charter schools, for-profit educational alternative companies, home schooling, and voucher programs that would support private schools serve as options to a general public that is fed-up with poor performing public schools.

Discussion about the school leadership shortage must take into account the role of the *public* in public education. In the current environment, as the significance of education grows along with educational options for parents, educators will need to do a better job of communicating to the public about the *value* of what public schools do. This need cannot be taken for granted.

CONCLUSION

In his study on school teacher job satisfaction Firestone (1994) discusses the significance of the intrinsic and extrinsic factors of a job. Intrinsic factors have to do with "the work itself." Individuals must believe they are having a desired impact. Job satisfaction comes from knowing you are accomplishing what you set out to do (i.e., change the school climate, improve student achievement, enhance high teacher morale, etc.). Extrinsic factors have more to do with income or compensation issues. In this respect, it is possible to earn a substantial income (extrinsic factor) and be miserable because you feel that you have little control over what occurs in your job (intrinsic factor). Preliminary data on the school administrative shortage shows serious problems along both intrinsic and extrinsic job dimensions. Compensation and job stress have been cited over and over again as the primary reasons why people lack interest in the school administration profession.

Discussion about bringing policy solutions to the school administrator shortage dilemma must consider internal changes to the profession. This discussion should be guided by why teachers are less likely to enter the administrative profession, as well as concern with why individuals hold administrative licenses but do not secure jobs in school administration. Administrator retention issues must be addressed as this relates to terminations, retirement, lateral transfers, and job burnout. Preparation and professional development must be included in a policy discussion about the profession of school administration. Individuals who are not properly prepared will not survive. The constant changes in the school environment and desires among multiple stakeholders in the community require strategies for ensuring that ongoing professional development is institutionalized in the administrative field.

As the importance of education continues to grow in an increasingly complex global economy, the job of the school administrator becomes more complex. This growing complexity means that school administrators must become more adept at communicating with multiple constituency groups and individuals in a given community. In this regard, policy-related discussion must include suggestions about building the profession as this relates to external (the community) development factors. Under the rubric of an educational ecosystem, how can school leaders work effectively with leadership at all levels of a given community to advance student achievement?

NOTES

1.   The NPBEA Policy Circle is comprised of research representatives of seven university-based educational policy centers from across the United States. One of the major purposes of the NPBEA Policy Circle is to conduct research on issues that are of vital importance to the NPBEA organizational membership. The NPBEA membership consists of the chief executive officers of the American Association of Colleges for Teacher Education, American Association of School Administrators, Association for Supervision and

Curriculum Development, Council of Chief State Officers, National Association of Elementary School Principals, National Association of Secondary School Principals, National Council of Professors of Educational Administration, National School Boards Association, and the University Council for Educational Administration.

2. See Weis, L., & Fine, M. (1993). *Beyond silenced voices: Class, race, and gender in United States schools*. New York: SUNY Press.

3. See Kaplan, G. R. (November, 1996). Profits R us: Notes on the commercialization of America's schools. *Phi Delta Kappan*, 1–12.

REFERENCES

Abrell, R. (1984). Leading by stepping down. *The Clearinghouse, 57*, 351–352.

Armstrong, W. I. (1990). Retention incentives: A necessity of the 1990's? *School Business Affairs, 56*, 40–42.

Bowles, B. D. (1990). The silent crisis in educational leadership. *The Education Digest, 55*, 12–14.

Chand, K. (1990). *Pressures, stresses, anxieties, and on job safety of the school superintendents*. (ED321421). Washington, DC: Educational Resources Information Center.

Crawford, J. (1998). (Discussion Paper). Changes in administrative licensure: 1991–1996. Columbia, MO: University Council for Educational Administration.

Domenech, D. A. (1996). Surviving the ultimate stress. *The School Administrator, 32*, 40–41.

Feistritzer, E. C. (1988). Point: "A good ole boy mentality rules your schools." *The Executive Educator, 10*(5), 24–37.

Firestone, W. A. (1994). Incentives for teachers: Mixing the intrinsic with the financial. In B.A. Jones & K. M. Borman (Eds.) *Investing in U. S. Schools: Directions for Educational Policy* (pp: 53–67). Norwood, NJ: Ablex Publishing Corporation.

Forsyth, P., & Jones, B. A. (1998, November). *Assuring the supply of quality leaders for America's schools: A vital concern*. Paper presented at National Policy Board for Educational Administration "Policy Circle" Summit. Columbia, MO: National Policy Board for Educational Administration.

Gmelch, W. H. (1996, March). Breaking out of superintendent stress traps. *The School Administrator, 32*, 32–33.

Goodlad, J. I. (1994). *A Place Called School*. New York: McGraw Hill.

Hartocollis, A. (1999, May 27). Giuliani calls for removing principals. *Education Week, XVIII*(37), 7.

Hess, F. (1988). When our veteran superintendents retire, who'll step into their shoes? *The School Administrator, 32*, 43–44.

Hodgkinson, H. L., & Montenegro, X. (1999). *The U.S. School Superintendent: The Invisible C.E.O.* Washington, DC: Institute for Educational Leadership.

Houston, P. D. (1998, June 3). The ABCs of administrative shortages. *Education Week, XVII*(38), 44.

Hudson, M. J. (1994). Women and minorities in school administration: Re-examining the role of *informal* job contact systems. *Urban Education, 28*(4), 386–397.

Johnson, J. (1987). School administrator supply and demand for the state of Maine. (ED306654). Gorham: University of Southern Maine Testing and Assessment Center.

Jones, B. A. (1994). The "multiple constituency" concept of collaboration: Influences of race, class, gender, and ethnicity. *Theory Into Practice, 33*(4), 226–234.

Keller, B. (1998a, March 18). Principals' shoes are hard to fill, study finds. *Education Week.*

Keller, B. (1998b, November 11). Principal matters. *Education Week.*

Krieger, N., & Sidney, S. (1996). Racial discrimination and blood pressure: The CARDIA study of young black and white adults. *American Journal of Public Health, 86*(10), 1370–1378.

Light, K. C., Brownley, K. A., Turner, J. R., Hinderliter, A. L., Girdler, S. S., Sherwood, A., & Anderson, N. B. (1995). Job status and high-effort coping influence work blood pressure in women and blacks. *Hypertension, 25*(4), 554–559.

McCormick, K. (1987). The school executive shortage: How serious is it? *The Education Digest, 53*, 2–5.

McLaughlin, M. W. (1998). *Strategies for fixing failing public schools.* Cambridge: Pew Charitable Trust (Forum on Standards-Based Reform).

Murphy, J. (1999, April). *Implementation of interstate school leaders licensure consortium standards.* Paper presented at annual meeting of the American Educational Research Association. Montreal, Canada.

National Association of Elementary School Principals (1998). *Is there a shortage of qualified candidates for openings in the principalship? An exploratory study.* Arlington, VA: Educational Research Service.

O'Connor, P., & Stearns, M. (1999, July 7). "No" shakes KC district again. *The Kansas City Star,* A1, A8.

Olson, L. (1999, April). Help wanted. *Teacher Magazine*, 1–3.

Pawlas, G. (1989). Supply and demand trends for elementary school administrators in South Carolina from 1977–2002. (ED320194).

Shakeshaft, C. (1998). Wild patience and bad fit: Assessing the impact of affirmative action on women in school administration. *Educational Researcher, 27*(9), 10–12.

Spaulding, W. B. (1954). *The superintendency of public schools: An anxious profession.* Cambridge: Harvard University Press.

Tallerico, M., Burstyn, J. N., & Poole, W. (1993). Gender and politics at work: Why women exit the superintendency. Fairfax, Virginia: National Policy Board for Educational Administration.

Tallerico, M., Poole, W., & Burstyn, J. N. (1994). Exits from urban superintendencies: The intersection of politics, race, and gender. *Urban Education, 28*(4), 439–454.

Torelli, J. A., & Gmelch, W. H. (1993). Occupational stress and burnout in educational administration. *People and Education, 1*(4), 363–381.

Trotter, A. (1999, March 3). Demand for principals growing but candidates aren't applying. *Education Week.*

United States Department of Education, NCES (1997). *Public and private school principals in the United States: A statistical profile, 1987–88 to 1993–94.* Washington, DC: United States Department of Education.

White, K. A. (1999, March 3). Power shift for Detroit moves ahead. *Education Week.*

Willie, C. V., Rieker, P. P., Krammer, B. M., & Brown, B. S. (1995). *Mental health, racism, and sexism.* Pittsburgh: University of Pittsburgh Press.

AUTHOR INDEX

SUBJECT INDEX